JON ★ BONNELL'S
TEXAS
Favorites

JON ★ BONNELL'S

TEXAS

Favorites

JON BONNELL

PHOTOGRAPHS BY B. J. LACASSE

GIBBS SMITH
TO ENRICH AND INSPIRE HUMANKIND

To my wife, Melinda.

You've taken this crazy journey of a chef's life with me so gracefully and patiently, I cannot begin to say thank you enough. You keep me grounded, motivated and constantly laughing. I also dedicate this book to our two beautiful kids, Charlotte and Rick. If I can teach either one to cook, we may just have a retirement plan in about 18 years!

First Edition
16 15 14 13 12   5 4 3 2 1

Text © 2012 Jon Bonnell
Photographs © 2012 by B. J. Lacasse

Published by
Gibbs Smith
P.O. Box 667
Layton, Utah 84041

1.800.835.4993 orders
www.gibbs-smith.com

Designed by Michelle Farinella
Printed and bound in China
Gibbs Smith books are printed on either recycled, 100% post-consumer waste, FSC-certified papers or on paper produced from sustainable PEFC-certified forest/controlled wood source. Learn more at www.pefc.org.

Library of Congress Cataloging-in-Publication Data

Bonnell, Jon.
  Jon Bonnell's Texas favorites / Jon Bonnell ;
photographs by B. J. Lacasse. — 1st ed.
      p. cm.
  Includes index.
  ISBN 978-1-4236-2259-8
1. Cooking, American—Southwestern style. 2. Cooking—Texas. I. Title.
  TX715.2.S69B665 2012
  641.59764—dc23
                                    2011038365

✪ Contents

Acknowledgments

I'd like to thank B. J. Lacasse for all of her hard work on the photography in this book and for her patience and understanding as my team took over her house while we staged each photo in her studio. I'd also like to thank Chefs Ed McOwen and James Pallett for helping to develop, test and photograph each dish. I could not ask for finer professionals to work with. Big thanks also to my wife, Melinda, and Chelsie Thornton for keeping this A.D.D. chef on-task and organized—both monumental challenges.

I also want to thank the farmers, ranchers, cheesemakers and other artisans who work tirelessly to bring the finest ingredients to my kitchen each and every day. Without their dedication to quality, my job would not be possible. I've always kept a "no secrets" policy in my kitchen, giving away all recipes and sources for products. Here are a few of the incredible suppliers who keep my kitchen stocked with all of the finest that Texas has to offer.

★ B & G Garden Produce
★ Brazos Valley Cheesemakers
★ Broken Arrow Ranch Venison Products
★ Burgundy Pasture Beef
★ Comanche Buffalo
★ Copper Shoals Redfish Farm
★ Cox's Farm Produce
★ Diamond H Ranch Quail Farm
★ Dominion Farms Free Range Chicken, Eggs and Pork
★ Eagle Mountain Farmhouse Cheesemakers
★ Frontier Meats Wild and Exotic Game Processing
★ Frugé Aquafarms
★ Generation Farms Fresh Herbs
★ Grandpa's Blueberry Patch
★ The Homestead Gristmill
★ La Casa Verde Hydroponics
★ Latte Da Goat Dairy and Cheesemakers
★ M & M Orchard and Farm
★ Metro Bakery
★ The Mozzarella Company
★ Pendery's World of Chiles & Spices
★ Scott Farms Produce
★ Selective Seasonings
★ Strube Ranch Wagyu Beef
★ Sweet Adeline's Organics
★ Texas Heritage Beef
★ Tin Top Farms Produce
★ Veldhuizen Cheesemakers
★ Worthington Orchards
★ Young's Greenhouse Baby Lettuces

Introduction

As a professional chef, I'm often asked, "What do you cook when you're at home?" I obviously don't pull off complicated dishes every night for the family, but that doesn't mean the food in my house is boring by any means. I tend to stick with the classic cuisine that I grew up cooking and eating with my family (every dish, of course, tweaked a little over the years). There are occasions like elaborate dinner parties or special celebrations when it's fun to pull out the stops, but on a regular basis I tend to keep it on the simple side.

In my first cookbook, *Fine Texas Cuisine,* I wanted to share the recipes and dishes that have made my fine dining restaurant the *Zagat* highest-rated restaurant in the state of Texas. In this book, however, I've decided to put together a collection of recipes for dishes that are easier for the home cook to pull off. This is the kind of stuff that I cook when no one is looking.

After fifteen years in the food industry, I still maintain a completely "no secrets" approach to everything I cook. I'm more than happy to give away every recipe that I have ever developed and help customers source rare or exotic ingredients when they are trying something difficult at home. As a former teacher, I just can't help sharing my experience and knowledge, and I wish every "foodie" that loves to cook at home all of the success in the world. Customers often contact me for problem-solving tips

as well, which I encourage. Anyone who's looking for a recipe or is having trouble making one work has only to send me an email via *bonnellstexas.com,* and I'm more than happy to respond right back with answers and tips. I love having this sense of transparency in what I cook.

In my first book I gave away the recipes to the two different spice blends that I use on a regular basis. I have since bottled both of those blends and sell them from my website, *bonnellstexas.com,* and in many grocery stores. The brand name for my spice blends is Texas Red Dirt Rub; I make one Creole blend and one Southwestern blend. The term "spice" to me means so much more than just heat. Spice, given just the right complexity, can dramatically improve the flavor of so many things when used appropriately. I strive for balance, intensity, bold flavor and proper levels of heat in my spice blends, rather than just adding fire to food.

I also use a lot of different types of "chili powder" in my dishes. This generic term is an oversimplified name for something that we take very seriously in Texas. I buy almost all of my chili powders from Pendery's World of Chiles & Spices here in Fort Worth and truly believe in the quality of their products. Their chili powder blends vary in heat level as well as intensity and are well worth exploring.

Tex-Mex Essentials

It's been joked that the recipe for a decent guacamole is printed on the back of all Texas birth certificates.

The flavors of Texas have been influenced by Mexican fare probably more than any other cuisine. The abundance of chiles, tortillas, salsas and the like can be found in virtually any city in the Lone Star State. When I left my home state for different schools and jobs (all quite far away), I probably missed the Mexican food more than any other comforts of home.

When we refer to Mexican food in Texas, we pretty much always mean Tex-Mex. Tex-Mex is not quite authentic Mexican cuisine, although some very traditional Mexican techniques and flavors do make their way into the mix. It's a version of Mexican that has evolved over the years into something all its own. You just can't get good Tex-Mex anywhere else, not the way we do it. And while Tex-Mex can vary drastically around the state from Laredo to Amarillo, the basics are pretty standard statewide. This chapter can get you started in the area of Tex-Mex basics no matter where you currently reside.

Homemade Flour Tortillas

2 cups flour
1 teaspoon kosher salt
2 tablespoons butter
3 tablespoons lard
1/2 cup room-temperature water
1 1/2 teaspoons olive oil

In a large mixing bowl, combine flour and salt and mix thoroughly. Add butter and lard in pieces and cut in with a pastry cutter until the mixture has a fine grainy texture. (This can be done with just your fingertips if you do not have a pastry cutter.) Place the dough in a food processor and turn on while pouring in water and oil. As soon as a ball begins to form, remove dough from the processor and turn out onto a cutting board dusted with flour. Cut the dough into 10 equal parts and cover with plastic wrap. Allow the dough to rest for 1 hour, then roll out with a pastry dowel or rolling pin into 6–8-inch tortillas. Cook on a cast-iron surface or nonstick griddle or pan at approximately 375 degrees until lightly browned and bubbly. This should take about 45 seconds per side. Set aside and cover with a kitchen towel and keep warm until ready to serve.

Makes 10 tortillas

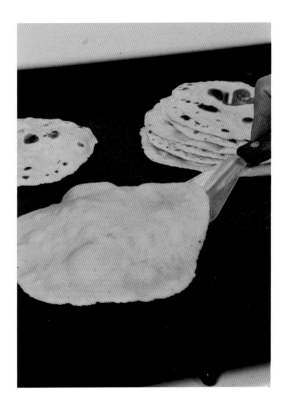

 Fresh homemade flour tortillas are a labor of love. It can be somewhat tricky to get the hang of them the first time, but once you've made a perfect tortilla, you'll never forget it. The ingredients are simple, but the technique can take some experimenting to figure out.

Homemade Corn Tortillas

2 cups dry masa harina
1 ounce lard
1 teaspoon kosher salt
1 1/2 cups warm water

Mix all ingredients by hand in a large mixing bowl until a ball has formed, then turn onto a cutting board and knead for 2–3 minutes, until the dough is completely uniform. Cover tightly with plastic wrap and let rest for 30 minutes. Divide the dough into 12 equal parts and make into tortillas using a tortilla press. For best results, cover both sides of the press with plastic to keep the dough from sticking. Heat a cast-iron or nonstick griddle to 375 degrees and cook each tortilla for 30 seconds per side, until lightly browned and puffy. Keep warm until ready to serve.

Makes 12 tortillas

 For corn tortillas, the dough has to be just right and the heat on the griddle has to be precise to get the tortillas to lightly puff up when cooked. Dry masa is very common and easy to find, but if you are lucky enough to have a supplier of fresh masa, your tortillas will taste even better. This recipe uses dry. The tortilla press is the easiest way to get the perfect thickness for corn tortillas, but a rolling pin can also be used.

Fresh Simple Salsa

2 pounds fresh red-ripe
    tomatoes, cores removed

1 small sweet onion (approximately
    5 ounces), peeled

Juice of 3 limes

2 fresh jalapeño peppers,
    diced (seeds optional)*

2 large cloves garlic, peeled

2 1/2 teaspoons kosher salt

1/4 teaspoon freshly ground
    black pepper

6–8 sprigs fresh cilantro

Cut all vegetables into large random chunks, then run all of the ingredients (starting with the cilantro) through a grinder with the medium-sized grinder plate installed. Season with salt and pepper. Whisk the salsa to combine then let sit refrigerated for 1 hour before tasting. Make any corrections necessary to seasonings and serve immediately.

Makes 6 cups

*Including the seeds from the jalapeños will give this salsa a nice little spicy kick, but the heat can be adjusted by removing the seeds if desired. The vast majority of the heat in a fresh jalapeño is contained in the white veins that hold the seeds. Basically, any part of the jalapeño colored white has the most heat, while the dark green parts have the most flavor. Remove all or some of the veins to adjust the heat level to your desired taste.

I love this great simple fresh salsa during the summer and fall, when the tomatoes are in perfect season. I leave in the skins and seeds for this rustic dish.

The key to a great salsa sometimes comes down to simplicity and a proper balance of acidity, sweetness, heat and salt. The grinder is the perfect tool for this salsa because of the uniform texture that it's capable of producing. It can be made in a food processor or blender, but I love the texture that only a grinder can produce. The taste will be a direct reflection of the quality and ripeness of the fresh tomatoes. My personal favorite for this recipe is the porter tomato, but I love to shop the local farmers market for the best tomatoes in season on any given day. The best tomatoes will always be the homegrown varieties that have a strong smell and slightly soft feel. Hard tomatoes with no odor and little color will have very little flavor, and truth be told, I'd rather use canned tomatoes than sub-par generic fresh ones.

Roasted Salsa Verde

2 pounds fresh tomatillos,
   husks removed, washed
2 poblano peppers
1 small sweet onion (Texas
   1015 is preferred), diced
2 fresh jalapeños, diced
   (seeds optional)
2 cloves garlic, roughly chopped
2 cups chicken stock or
   vegetable stock
$^1/_2$ teaspoon vegetable oil
$^3/_4$ teaspoon salt
2–3 cracks of freshly ground
   black pepper
Juice of 1$^1/_2$ limes
6–8 sprigs fresh cilantro, chopped

Roast the tomatillos over an open flame or grill until browned on all sides. Roast the poblanos as well until all sides are black. (This can be done under a broiler, but an open flame or grill is recommended.) Once the tomatillos are browned lightly on all sides, place into a large mixing bowl, retaining all juices.

Allow the poblanos to sweat in a paper bag or plastic bag for 15 minutes, or until cool enough to handle, then scrape off the black skin using the back edge of a knife. Remove the seeds and stem and roughly chop. Add the flesh of the pepper to the mixing bowl.

In a medium-sized saucepot, sauté the onions, jalapeño and garlic in oil just until soft, then add in all remaining ingredients except for the lime juice and cilantro. Be sure to add in all of the juice from the roasted tomatillos. Simmer the mixture for 20–30 minutes on low, then puree with a stick blender until smooth. Add the lime juice and chopped cilantro at the very end, and taste for seasoning balance.

Make 6 cups

Salsa Verde is one of the basics of any Tex-Mex kitchen and has incredible versatility. In addition to just a simple dip, it also makes a great base for green chili when added to browned diced pork with sliced onion and peppers, or it can be used as the base for many different types of casseroles. The combined smell of roasting chiles and tomatillos on the grill and fresh tortillas on the flat-top emanates from every Mexican restaurant in Texas. After having lived in various other parts of the country for almost twelve years, this was the kind of familiar aroma that let me know I was home.

Fresh Salsa Verde

1 bunch fresh cilantro,
   most stems removed
1 pound tomatillos, husks
   removed, washed
2 cloves garlic, peeled
1 large shallot, peeled
3 large jalapeños, seeds
   and veins removed
1 serrano pepper, seeds removed
Juice of 2 limes
2 teaspoons kosher salt
Pinch of freshly ground
   black pepper

Roughly chop cilantro, tomatillos, garlic, shallot, serrano, and jalapeños into large pieces; run them all through a grinder with the medium-sized grinder plate installed, starting with the cilantro. Add the lime juice, salt, and pepper, and whisk the salsa to combine. Allow to sit refrigerated for at least 1 hour before tasting.

Makes 2¹/₂ cups

 The tart green flavors of this salsa just scream out summer to me. This is the kind of salsa I love to have around when throwing parties by the pool. It works as a simple dip with chips and also goes well over eggs or makes a delicious condiment for any number of different tacos. Unlike the earthy and complex cooked version of salsa verde, this recipe is bright with fresh acidic green flavors.

Smoky Salsa with Chile Mora

2 cups water

1 small sweet onion (approximately 6 ounces), peeled and halved

1 jalapeño pepper, stem removed

4 large cloves garlic, peeled

2 mora chiles, stems and seeds removed

2 pounds fresh red-ripe tomatoes, cores removed

4–5 sprigs fresh cilantro, chopped

Juice of 2 limes

2 teaspoons kosher salt

$^{1}/_{4}$ teaspoon freshly ground black pepper

In a small saucepot, add the water, onion, jalapeño, garlic and mora chiles. Bring to a simmer. Simmer lightly for 10–12 minutes, until the onions have softened and the chiles are completely rehydrated.

Grill the tomatoes over an open flame until lightly charred on all sides, then add to the simmering pot. Cook together for 3–4 minutes. Remove all ingredients from the pot with a slotted spoon and place in a food processor or blender. Add cilantro, lime juice, salt, and pepper. Pulse a few times until smooth. Serve warm or cool.

Makes 6 cups

This salsa has a slightly more complex flavor profile than most. A mora chile is a ripe red jalapeño that has been smoked and dried. The morita is similar but slightly smaller and usually derived from the serrano pepper instead of the jalapeño. Similar to chipotles, moras have a rich, sweet, smoky characteristic that really adds a rustic touch to salsas and soups. Though not always easy to find, moras can always be ordered from specialty stores like Pendery's and are worth seeking out. This dish can be made with chipotles, but I greatly prefer moras or moritas.

Rustic Ranch Salsa

1 large purple onion
2 pounds firm red tomatoes,
   cores removed
1 ear fresh corn
2 poblano peppers
3 fresh jalapeño peppers
Juice of 2 limes
1/4 teaspoon ground coriander
Pinch of ground cumin
Pinch of garlic powder
Pinch of onion powder
Pinch of brown sugar
1/2 teaspoon ground black pepper
2 teaspoons kosher salt

Slice the onion into large rings and grill until very well charred. Char the tomatoes just until the skins have lightly blackened, and then remove to a mixing bowl with the onions. Be sure to keep all of the juices from the tomatoes and onions.

Remove the husk from the corn and grill lightly on all sides until many of the kernels are golden brown or charred. Cut the kernels from the cob and keep separate from the other ingredients until the end.

Roast the poblanos and jalapeños until the skins are black. Allow them to sweat in a paper bag or sealed plastic bag for 10–15 minutes, until cool enough to handle. Remove the skins by scraping off with the back of a knife blade; remove and discard the seeds and stems as well.

Add the peppers and all of the remaining ingredients, except corn, to the bowl. In small batches, place the contents into a food processor and pulse lightly just until the salsa has a chunky consistency. Do not puree all the way to a smooth texture. After pulsing all of the salsa, add in the corn; mix and serve. This salsa is great served chunky style with fresh tortilla chips.

Makes 6 cups

 This is a heartier and more robust salsa than most, with plenty of Tex-Mex flavor and just enough kick, balanced by a touch of sweet.

Pico de Gallo

1 small onion, finely diced

4 Roma tomatoes, seeds
    removed, finely diced

2 large jalapeño peppers, seeds
    removed, finely diced

2 tablespoons lime juice

2 tablespoons chopped cilantro

$1/4$ teaspoon freshly ground
    black pepper

$1\,1/4$ teaspoons kosher salt

Combine all ingredients except salt, and let sit for 30–45 minutes. Add the salt just before serving.

Makes 2 cups

 Pico de gallo is one of the simplest, most satisfying and most common staples of Texas and Mexican cooking. It's a perfect condiment for any number of dishes and even works as a simple dip for corn chips. One common mistake is adding the salt in this dish too early. Pico can be made a day ahead of time if desired, but adding the salt early will draw all of the juices out of the tomatoes and onions and create a soupy mess. Pico should have a crisp and chunky texture, never mushy or watery.

Smooth and Creamy Guacamole

2 large ripe Hass avocados
1 large jalapeño, stem removed
(seeds optional)
1 large clove fresh garlic, peeled
2 teaspoons chopped cilantro
1 tablespoon lime juice
$^1/_2$ teaspoon kosher salt
Pinch of ground black pepper

Place all ingredients into a food processor or food-grade blender and puree until completely smooth. Serve immediately!

Makes 1$^1/_2$ cups

 This is one of those staples in my life that I can hardly image living without. We use it so often at the restaurant that we never have the problem of the avocado turning brown. If you intend to make this ahead of time, press a sheet of plastic wrap all the way down on the surface of the guac and keep it in the fridge. Depending on the avocados used, it can last up to 24 hours but will be at its peak in the first several hours after being made.

Chunky Traditional Guacamole

2 large ripe Hass avocados
1 large fresh jalapeño
3 tablespoons minced onion
1 Roma tomato, seeded
    and finely diced
Juice of 1 1/2 limes
1/2 teaspoon kosher salt
Pinch of garlic powder
Pinch of ground black pepper
1 tablespoon chopped cilantro

Place all ingredients into a mixing bowl and smash the avocado roughly with a fork until all ingredients are combined, yet still slightly chunky. Serve immediately!

Makes 1 1/2 cups

This is the most broadly recognized version of guacamole. Many restaurants serve this dish with tableside preparation to show off their use of ripe avocados and the freshest ingredients. It's never acceptable to make this dish a day or two ahead of time. Perfectly ripe avocados are sacred and must be eaten quickly, before their fragile contents begin to brown and bitter. All of the prep work can be done well ahead of time, but once you cut into an avocado, it's time to mix, taste (for me, tasting several times) and serve, no waiting.

The key to making good guac (as it's often called in Texas) is the proper balance of acidity, salt and spice. Bland guac can be almost tasteless but is easily brought to life with just a squeeze of lime and more salt. The heat level will be determined by the jalapeños in this recipe. For young kids, they can be completely de-seeded to make the dish extremely mild, or for the seasoned veteran, leave the entire contents in there for more kick. It's even common to serve guac like this with the jalapeños on the side.

Molcajete Guacamole
with Hatch Chiles

1 small sweet onion
2 hot Hatch chiles
1 large fresh jalapeño
1 Roma tomato
1 teaspoon kosher salt
Juice of 1 1/2 limes
1 tablespoon chopped cilantro
2 large ripe Hass avocados
Pinch of garlic powder
Pinch of ground cumin
Pinch of ground coriander
Pinch of ground black pepper

Slice the onion into thick rounds and grill over an open flame until charred on both sides, then roughly chop it. Roast the Hatch chiles and jalapeño until the skins blacken, then allow to sweat for 10–15 minutes in a paper bag or sealed plastic bag. Scrape the skins off with the back of a knife and remove the seeds. Roughly chop the chiles. Cut the tomato in half lengthwise and grill, skin side down, until the skins are nicely charred. In a molcajete,* begin with the chiles, onion and salt. Work the ingredients with the stone against the edges of the bowl to begin breaking them down, but do not completely puree the ingredients. They should be ground into large rustic pieces. Once this is achieved, add the lime, tomatoes and cilantro and continue to grind. Add avocado in last with the remaining spices and mix until well blended.

Makes 1 1/2–2 cups

**A molcajete is a large rustic type of mortar and pestle.*

A good molcajete is a wonderful piece of equipment that adds an almost indescribable element to anything prepared in it. There is something magical that happens when food is ground by hand across rough stone. The cheapest versions are made from cement and will always leave pieces of grit in your dishes, no matter how long you use them. The best type is ground from one piece of pure basalt, with no filler added whatsoever. When it's brand new, it needs to be seasoned before using. One popular way to season a molcajete is to place a half-cup of dry rice into it and grind until it becomes almost a powder; then clean the molcajete with cold water and it should be ready to go.

Fajitas for the Family

MARINADE

¼ cup pineapple juice

1 tablespoon Worcestershire sauce

2 tablespoons soy sauce

Juice of 1 lemon

2 chipotles (canned in adobo sauce)

6–8 sprigs cilantro

1 teaspoon dried Mexican oregano

½ teaspoon ground cumin

½ teaspoon ground coriander

4 large cloves garlic, peeled

1 teaspoon onion powder

3 tablespoons vegetable oil

4 ounces Shiner Bock beer*

Combine all ingredients, except beer, in a blender and puree until completely smooth. Mix the beer in last. Be sure to remove the center cap in the blender top and cover with a towel to keep the beer from blowing off the lid. Pour over beef to marinate.

FAJITAS

2 pounds skirt or flank steak

1 tablespoon Texas Red Dirt Rub
      Southwestern Blend**

1 large sweet onion, sliced
      into thick rings

2 poblano peppers, seeds
      removed, cut into rings

*The rest of the bottle is for the cook.

**This is my own special blend. Buy it at the restaurant or online.

Trim the beef of the silver skin and as much of the fat as you can. Place in a ziplock bag and pour in the marinade. Seal and let marinate in the fridge for at least 3 hours or overnight. Remove the beef from the fridge and grill to desired temperature over a hardwood fire, dusting with Texas Red Dirt Rub on both sides. Once the beef is cooked, remove from heat and let rest for 5 minutes before cutting.

Grill the onion rings and peppers over the fire until well caramelized, dusting lightly with the Red Dirt Rub. Scatter the onions and peppers on a large platter, slice the beef thinly across the grain of the meat, and then place the beef on top. Serve the platter in the middle of the table with warm flour tortillas and your favorite sides.

Serves 6–8

POPULAR SIDES FOR FAJITAS

Guacamole

Sprigs of fresh cilantro

Pico de Gallo (see page 20)

Salsa

Shredded cheese

Sour cream

Chopped jalapeños

A huge pile of freshly grilled fajita meat, served on a sizzling platter steaming with freshly squeezed lime juice is the heart and soul of most Mexican restaurants in Texas. You can hear your food coming all the way from the kitchen and the aroma fills the entire dining room. The word fajita *comes from the Spanish word for belt, where the skirt steak comes from on a cow; so technically, there is no such thing as a chicken fajita or a mushroom fajita. That being said, this recipe is also great for chicken and is very commonly served (even though incorrectly) in most Mexican restaurants as an alternative to beef. A fresh hot flour tortilla slathered with guacamole, a few strips of grilled onion, 3–4 slices of fajita meat and a spoonful of pico is truly my number-one comfort food.*

Tamales take a while to perfect, but once you have your technique down, they are a treasure to be shared with friends and family. It's tradition to make tamales around the holidays and give them away by the dozen. These tamales also freeze well, so make plenty.

Green Tamales

CORN HUSKS

1 (8-ounce) package dried
    corn husks (may contain
    up to 100 husks, so be
    prepared to make plenty)

TAMALE DOUGH

1 cup yellow corn grits (stone
    ground, not instant)
2 3/4 cups chicken stock
1 1/2 teaspoons salt
1/2 teaspoon ground coriander
1/2 teaspoon garlic powder
1/2 teaspoon onion powder
1/2 teaspoon chili powder
    (preferably ancho)
1 1/4 cups dry masa harina
8 tablespoons (4 ounces) lard
1/2 teaspoon baking powder
8 tablespoons (one stick) butter

CHICKEN FILLING

1 pound shredded smoked chicken
2 cups Roasted Salsa Verde
    (see page 14)

Boil the husks in water, covered, for 8–10 minutes, then let sit in the hot water for 45 minutes to 1 hour. Once they are soft and pliable, they are ready to use. Tear the first few into long strips for tying.

To make the dough, place the grits in a food processor or spice grinder and pulse until the large pieces have somewhat broken down. In a saucepot, bring the chicken stock and all dry seasonings to a boil. Whisk the grits into the hot stock, then cook at a light simmer for 5 minutes, stirring frequently. Remove from heat, cover and let stand for 15 minutes. Add the masa harina and whisk until incorporated fully, then let cool to room temperature. In a stand mixer using the paddle attachment, whip the lard, baking powder and butter until creamy, about 2–3 minutes; then add in the masa mixture a little at a time until the whole batch reaches a thick batter consistency. If the batter becomes too thick, adjust with a little chicken stock.

Spread out the soft corn husks and spoon 4–5 tablespoons of the tamale dough onto the center of each. Spread the dough around with the back of a spoon, leaving at least a 1-inch gap around all of the edges to save room for rolling. Place a heaping spoonful of shredded smoked chicken in the center of each, topped with one spoonful of Roasted Salsa Verde. Roll the tamales first from the sides towards the middle, covering the filling with the dough; then fold the long ends towards the center and tie shut with torn strips of corn husk. Line the tamales in a steamer basket and let steam for 1 1/2 hours. Let rest for 10–15 minutes before serving, or freeze for later.

Makes 12–14 tamales

Tips for non-Texans: Be sure to remove the corn husk before eating. The husk is just the wrapper, not really edible for humans. When it's time to make tamales, it's usually worth making a lot while you have all the ingredients on hand and sharing with family and friends. Tamales can be topped with your favorite salsa, chili, or melted cheese or just enjoyed alone. If corn husks aren't available, banana leaves are a good alternative.

Red Tamales

CORN HUSKS

1 (8-ounce) package dried
corn husks (may contain
up to 100 husks, so be
prepared to make plenty)

TAMALE DOUGH

1 cup yellow corn grits (stone
ground, not instant)
2 3/4 cups chicken stock
1 1/2 teaspoons salt
1/2 teaspoon ground coriander
1/2 teaspoon garlic powder
1/2 teaspoon onion powder
1/2 teaspoon chili powder
(preferably ancho)
1 1/4 cups dry masa harina
8 tablespoons (4 ounces) lard
1/2 teaspoon baking powder
8 tablespoons (one stick) butter

MEAT FILLING

1 pound Perfect Texas Brisket
(see page 125) or Pulled Pork
(see page 128), shredded
with a fork
2 cups Guajillo Chili Sauce
(see page 137)

Boil the husks in water, covered, for 8–10 minutes, then let sit in the hot water for 45 minutes to 1 hour. Once they are soft and pliable, they are ready to use. Tear the first few into long strips for tying.

To make the dough, place the grits in a food processor or spice grinder and pulse until the large pieces have somewhat broken down. In a saucepot, bring the chicken stock and all dry seasonings to a boil. Whisk the grits into the hot stock, then cook at a light simmer for 5 minutes, stirring frequently. Remove from heat, cover and let stand for 15 minutes. Add in the masa harina and whisk until incorporated fully, then let cool to room temperature. In a stand mixer using the paddle attachment, whip the lard, baking powder and butter until creamy, about 2–3 minutes; then add in the masa mixture a little at a time until the whole batch reaches a thick batter consistency. If the batter becomes too thick, adjust with a little chicken stock.

Spread out the soft corn husks and spoon 3 ounces (4 tablespoons) of the tamale dough onto the center of each. Spread the dough around with the back of a spoon, leaving at least a 1-inch gap around all of the edges to save room for rolling. Place a heaping spoonful of shredded meat in the center of each, topped with one spoonful of Guajillo Chili Sauce. Roll the tamales first from the sides towards the middle, covering the filling with the dough; then fold the long ends towards the center and tie shut with torn strips of corn husk. Line the tamales in a steamer basket and let steam for 1 1/2 hours. Let rest for 10–15 minutes before serving, or freeze for later.

Makes 12–14 tamales

Crab-Stuffed Jalapeños, page 45

Small Bites, Big Tastes

Texans like to entertain. We probably throw as many parties per capita as any other state, and we find new ways and reasons to entertain every day.

The standard cocktail party pretty much has to begin with food from the moment the first guests arrive, and the appetizers really set the tone for the night. I like to be somewhat creative when it comes to passed appetizers, because it's the first chance to make an impression on my guests. For more formal parties, I try to keep appetizers to one-handed bites that can easily be navigated while holding a beverage in the other hand, to keep guests from feeling awkward or intimidated. But for less formal gatherings, it's more than acceptable to allow guests to get their hands a little dirty.

Just because a passed appetizer is small and can usually be popped down in one bite, that's no excuse for anything bland or boring when it comes to flavor. Big, bold flavors with even a little spicy heat can be a great kickoff to a successful shindig. I like to start off parties with some flair and intense bites to remember.

Oyster Shooters with Serrano

Juice of 3 lemons
Juice of 2 limes
2 serrano peppers, seeds
    removed, finely diced
1 Roma tomato, seeds
    removed, finely diced
1 small shallot, minced
$^3/_4$ teaspoon Texas Red Dirt
    Rub Southwestern Blend
$^1/_2$ teaspoon salt
2 dozen fresh oysters*

In a mixing bowl, combine the citrus juices, peppers, tomato, shallots, Southwestern Blend, and salt; let sit for 25–30 minutes. Shuck the oysters and place them in the bowl to marinate 5–10 minutes. Place each oyster in a shot glass with a spoonful of the marinade and serve. They can also be served back in their shells, but this can get somewhat messy.

Serves 24

*The rule about good oysters only being available in months that end with "r" was written in the late 1700s and is no longer true. Great oysters can be purchased any day of the year. Different places around the country have better seasons than others, but somewhere today, someone is pulling beautiful oysters out of the sea. It's very important to know and trust your source before eating any raw shellfish (or raw anything, for that matter). I'm always happy to share my personal sources for ingredients if you have trouble finding great oysters in your area.

I love this particular dish as an appetizer on a hot summer day. The shooters can be served on ice or directly from the refrigerator. The serrano pepper has a decent level of heat that can be managed by the way the seeds are removed. Most of the heat in the pepper is located in the white veins that hold the seeds.

Tangy, salty and spicy foods like these shooters are a perfect choice for hot Texas days. That little bit of sweat that comes from eating spicy food can help to cool you off in the heat of summer. When you think about it, most spicy dishes come from cuisines known for heat. Mexican, Indian, Thai, Caribbean and Texas foods all have some level of heat in many of their most popular dishes.

Deviled Quail Eggs

1 chicken egg
1 dozen quail eggs
3 tablespoons mayonnaise
1 tablespoon Dijon mustard
Pinch of chipotle chili powder
Pinch of hot smoked paprika
Pinch of mustard powder
Pinch of kosher salt

Cook the chicken egg separate from the quail eggs, since the sizes require different cooking times. Start the chicken egg in cold water; bring to a boil and cook for 5 minutes at a rolling boil. Remove the pot from the heat and let sit for 10 minutes; then remove the egg to an ice water bath.

Place quail eggs in a medium-size pot and cover eggs with cold water. Bring to a boil and cook for 2 full minutes. Remove from the heat and let sit in the water for 10 minutes; then place the eggs in ice water to cool down. Peel all of the eggs, slice in half lengthwise and carefully remove the yolks. Add all of the yolks (chicken included) into a mixing bowl and combine with the remaining ingredients and mix well. Discard the chicken egg whites and save the quail egg whites for filling. Once the yolk mixture has been mixed well, place the contents into a small pastry bag with a star tip, or into the corner of a ziplock bag and pipe into the quail egg whites.

Serves 4–6

 These little appetizer bites are a real hit at parties—easy to make, easy to eat and big on flavor. They can be garnished any number of ways, from fresh leaves of cilantro (or micro cilantro) on top, to snipped chives, chive blossoms, crispy bacon or even a little tuft of caviar for special occasions.
The chipotle chili powder adds a kick of heat and smoky flavor.

Shrimp Ceviche in Mini Cucumber Cups

1 pound baby gulf shrimp,
    peeled and deveined
Juice of 8 limes, divided
1/2 ounce white tequila
1/4 cup minced purple onion
2 serrano peppers, seeds and
    veins removed, finely diced
4 radishes, finely diced
3/4 teaspoon Texas Red Dirt
    Rub Southwestern Blend
1 pound small seedless cucumbers
1 ripe avocado, finely diced

Blanch the shrimp in boiling water for 20 seconds, then chill in ice water to stop the cooking; remove from the ice bath after 2 minutes. Marinate the shrimp in the juice of 6 limes (about 8 tablespoons) for 3–4 hours in the refrigerator. Drain the juice and combine the shrimp with fresh juice from the remaining 2 limes, tequila, onion, serrano, and radish. Season with the Southwestern Blend and let marinate for 1 hour.

Cut the cucumbers (peeling optional) into 2-inch segments, then hollow each out with a melon baller or spoon, leaving the bottom intact to form a small bowl or cup. Add the diced avocado to the shrimp mixture at the last minute, then fill each cup with the ceviche mixture and serve.

Serves 8–10

Ceviche is the perfect dish to serve in the heat of a Texas summer. This ceviche has enough heat to bring a touch of sweat, but not enough to hurt anyone. This dish pairs extremely well with an ice-cold glass of sauvignon blanc. Choosing perfectly sized cucumbers is the key to this appetizer: if they are too big, the dish cannot be served as a passed appetizer; if too small, the cups won't hold enough ceviche.

I first served this dish at the James Beard House in New York City, of all places. The idea of a corn dog seemed a little odd to many folks up there, but one taste and they were hooked. This batter works just fine with a hot dog, too. The key to a great corn dog is a batter with just the right balance of crisp texture with sweet corn flavor and a golden brown crust.

Rabbit Corn Dogs with Rosemary Mustard

CORN DOGS

12 rabbit loins
Salt and pepper
$1/2$ cup flour
$1 1/2$ cups cornmeal
$1 1/2$ teaspoons baking powder
$1/2$ teaspoon baking soda
1 teaspoon sugar
$1/4$ teaspoon salt
Pinch of garlic powder
$1/3$ teaspoon cayenne pepper
2 eggs
$1 1/4$ cups buttermilk
Oil for deep-frying

Cut the rabbit loins into bite-size pieces, $1 1/2$ to 2 inches long, and season well with salt and pepper. Mix all dry ingredients together using a whisk. In a separate bowl, whisk together the eggs and buttermilk until well incorporated. Add the wet mix to the dry mixture and whisk until the batter becomes uniform and smooth. Pierce each piece of rabbit with a wooden skewer, dip into the batter and coat well, then deep-fry in oil at 350 degrees for 2 minutes, turning occasionally until the corn dogs are brown and crisp on all sides. Remove and drain on paper towels. Serve hot with Rosemary Mustard as a dipping sauce.

Serves 10–12

ROSEMARY MUSTARD

$2/3$ cup Dijon mustard
2 tablespoons sour cream
$1/4$ teaspoon kosher salt
$1/4$ teaspoon freshly ground black pepper
Pinch of cayenne pepper
1 tablespoon freshly chopped rosemary

Whisk all items together in a mixing bowl and serve.

Makes about $2/3$ cup

Crab Poppers with Cascabel-Lime Aioli

CRAB POPPERS

1 pound jumbo lump crabmeat
1 cup buttermilk
$^1/_2$ teaspoon kosher salt
1 egg
2 cups panko bread crumbs
4–5 fresh chives, chopped
Vegetable oil for deep-frying
Chopped chives for garnish

Pick through the crabmeat for any shell pieces, but leave the large chunks intact. Combine the buttermilk, salt and egg, and whisk together until the mixture is smooth. Drop the pieces of crab into the wet mixture to coat, then transfer directly into the panko crumbs. Mix until well coated on all sides. Deep-fry the crab pieces in 365-degree oil until golden brown, then drain on paper towels. Serve each crab popper on an individual spoon, or with toothpicks as a passed appetizer. Drizzle with Cascabel-Lime Aioli and garnish with chopped chives.

Serves 6–8

CASCABEL-LIME AIOLI

15 cascabel chiles, stems
    and seeds removed
2 egg yolks
2 tablespoons Dijon mustard
$^1/_2$ teaspoon cayenne pepper
1 bunch scallions, green
    parts only, chopped
Juice of 3 limes
$^1/_2$ teaspoon kosher salt
1 $^1/_2$ cups canola oil

Simmer the cascabels in just enough water to cover for 22–24 minutes, with a tight-fitting lid. Once they are soft, transfer chiles to a food processor along with 4 tablespoons (2 ounces) of the cooking water. Add in all remaining ingredients, except the oil, and blend for 1 minute. After 1 minute, drizzle in the oil slowly while the processor is running until the aioli has a slightly thick mayonnaise consistency. If it gets too thick, add a little more cooking liquid. If it seems too thin, add more oil while the processor is running. Cool and serve.

Makes 2 cups

This is a perfect small bite to start off a party, packed with flavor and just a touch of heat, but not so hearty that everyone fills up before the main course. I love to serve this dish when the blue crabs are plentiful and fresh, huge jumbo lump crabmeat is abundant. The poppers can be served on individual spoons or skewered with large toothpicks.

Grilled Lobster Tacos with Tarragon-Serrano Aioli

3 lobster tails (8 ounces each)
Olive oil for cooking
$1/3$ teaspoon Texas Red Dirt
   Rub Creole Blend
12 flour tortillas
1 cup shredded cabbage

Cut the lobster tails in half lengthwise and brush lightly with olive oil. Season with the Creole Blend on the flesh side, and grill on medium heat with the flesh side facing down for the first $1^{1/2}$ minutes. Turn the lobster tails over and continue to cook in the shell until the tails begin to simmer inside their shells. Once they are done, remove from heat and let sit until cool enough to handle. Remove meat from the shells and slice into large chunks. Serve on hot fresh tortillas with shredded cabbage and Tarragon-Serrano Aioli.

Serves 6

TARRAGON-SERRANO AIOLI

2 egg yolks
$1/2$ tablespoon Dijon mustard
2 serrano peppers, seeds removed
1 clove garlic
2 tablespoons finely chopped
   fresh tarragon
Juice of 2 lemons
1 cup cooked baby artichoke
   quarters (fresh is best, but
   canned will work quite well)
1 teaspoon kosher salt
2 cups canola oil

Place all ingredients, except oil, in a food processor, and blend for 1 minute. After 1 minute, drizzle in the oil slowly while the processor is running until the aioli has a slightly thick mayonnaise consistency. Cool and serve.

Makes 3 cups

 This is my favorite indulgent grill fare when it's time to impress some guests. Everyone loves to stand around a grill at parties, and the site of crimson bubbling lobster tails grilled in their shells just sets the mood for a perfect night. I like to pair this dish with a simple, crisp, unoaked chardonnay or Pinot Grigio.

Crab-Stuffed Jalapeños

3 slices bacon

12 jalapeños

3 ounces cream cheese

3 ounces Boursin cheese

8 ounces fresh lump crabmeat,
    picked through for shell pieces

1 tablespoon chopped fresh chives

Pinch of kosher salt

Pinch of ground black pepper

Chopped fresh chives for garnish

Cook the bacon slices until crispy and then break apart by hand into large bits; set aside. To prepare to cook on a vertical roasting rack, hollow out the inside of each jalapeño, being sure to get as much of the white veins and seeds out as possible.* Combine the cream cheese and Boursin cheese, season with salt and pepper and warm just slightly; stir until smooth and creamy. Fold in the cleaned crabmeat, being very careful not to break the large lumps. Clean the peppers and stuff each pepper with as much cheese-and-crab mixture as it will take, even overstuffing a little bit. Bake in a 425-degree oven for approximately 7–8 minutes, until the cheese mixture is bubbling and lightly browned. Top each pepper with bits of bacon and fresh chives just before serving.

Serves 6–8

Alternately halve the peppers and remove stems, seeds, and veins. Stuff and then roast on a baking sheet.

 I'm not sure when I saw the first commercially available jalapeño roaster, but I've been stuffing and serving this type of appetizer ever since. It's important to remove all of the seeds and veins first, to tame the heat of these famous little peppers, but there's even a tool called the jalapeño corer on the market now. This dish works well when cooked in the oven but can be even more fun if the roaster is placed right on top of an outdoor grill and cooked with the lid down until the peppers soften and the filling lightly bubbles.

Chili Biscuits

2 cups flour

2 teaspoons baking powder

Pinch of cayenne pepper

Pinch of kosher salt

1 1/4 cups (2 1/2 sticks) cold salted
   butter, cut into cubes

1 cup plus 2 tablespoons buttermilk

1/2 cup Venison Chili (see page 166)
   or True Texas Chili (see page 75)

1/2 cup grated cheddar cheese

In a large mixing bowl, combine all dry ingredients
and whisk until mixed thoroughly. Cut in the cubes
of butter by hand or with a pastry blender until the
texture is like wet sand. Pour in the buttermilk and mix
by hand until the dough just barely comes together.
Do not overmix or knead the dough, as the biscuits
will become chewy and tough. Turn the dough out
onto a board or countertop dusted lightly with flour.
Roll the dough out to approximately 1 1/2 inches thick.
Cut out biscuits with a small circular ring and place
on a greased baking sheet. Make a deep dimple in the
center of each biscuit with your finger, then fill each
with a spoonful of chili and top with cheese. Bake at
350 degrees for 12 minutes, or until the biscuits have
browned and are bubbling lightly.

Serves 10–12

*The first time I had chili biscuits was at my grandmother's house. Even big
elaborate parties seemed to always begin with passed trays of chili biscuits. This
recipe can make any size biscuit, from a full portion to bite-size versions, simply
by cutting the dough in different-sized circles and varying the amount of chili
spooned into the middle. To keep the dough from sticking to your circle cutters,
dip the cutter in flour before each cut.*

Spicy Pickled Okra

1 pound fresh okra pods

3 large fresh jalapeño peppers,
    sliced in half lengthwise

8 cloves garlic, chopped

5 cups white vinegar (5% acidity)

2 cups water

4 1/2 tablespoons pickling salt

2 tablespoons mustard seeds

12–14 whole black peppercorns

1 teaspoon dill seed

1/2 teaspoon celery seed

Clean and wash the okra and jalapeños well before beginning the recipe. Combine all other ingredients in a pot and bring to a boil. Cook at a rolling boil for 4 full minutes. Place the okra and jalapeños in a large mixing bowl. Pour the boiling brine over okra and cover with plastic wrap; let steep, covered, for 45 minutes. Pack the okra and jalapeños in pint jars, then fill the jars with brine. Refrigerate immediately. These are meant to be eaten within a few weeks and must be kept refrigerated. For a longer shelf life, the jars must be canned appropriately using boiling water and sanitary canning procedures.

Makes 2–3 pint jars

 Okra has a bad reputation for its slimy texture. Pickled okra has none of that slimy texture and retains all of its natural crunch and fresh flavor. These okra pickles go great with sandwiches, make a great garnish for a bloody Mary, or taste great just as a snack.

Okra is one of the easiest vegetables to grow. The only hard part is having to pick it every couple of days. If okra is left on the vine for more than a few days, it gets tough and fibrous and becomes completely inedible.

Family-Style Fiestas

The family dinner table is still a sacred thing in Texas.

In a modern world of cell phones, voicemail, and social networking, the only real form of communication that stays constant these days is dinner conversation across a family table. The glue that holds the entire family dining experience together is the food, the centerpiece of the table itself. When I think of my own childhood, much of what comes to mind are the smells, sounds, and memories from family dinners. The phone was not to be answered, the TV was turned off, and we used the proper utensils at a properly set table when we ate together. Family time was savored, and the dinner meal was the perfect time for real communication.

The food that my mother put out on a regular basis was nothing short of outstanding. It wasn't until I entered culinary school that I realized what it took to pull off great meals on such a regular basis, but now I appreciate her cooking more every day. Great family meals don't have to be complicated or sophisticated, but family is worth splurging on once in a while. Delicious food alone is the perfect excuse to put everything else on hold, even if just for an hour or so a few nights a week. When it comes to dining with the family, these are some of my favorite dishes to satisfy everyone—from the kids to the grandparents and every palate in between.

Lone Star Layered Dip

1 pound ground beef

1 teaspoon vegetable oil

1 tablespoon Texas Red Dirt Rub
Southwestern Blend, plus more
for dusting the sour cream

2 cups refried pinto beans

2 cups Smooth and Creamy
Guacamole (see page 21)

2 cups sour cream

2 cups shredded cheddar cheese

2 cups diced tomatoes

2 cups diced green onions

The size of your layered dip will completely depend on the size of the platter you intend to use for service. The layers should be roughly the same thickness.

Brown the ground beef in oil until well rendered. Season with Texas Red Dirt Rub, then remove from pan and allow to cool. Drain grease. In a wide shallow dish, begin spreading a layer of refried pinto beans on the bottom. Top that layer with an even layer of the seasoned ground beef. Spread out the guacamole layer next, followed by the sour cream (lightly dusted with Texas Red Dirt Rub), cheese, tomatoes, and onions. The top layer of tomatoes and onions can be arranged in any artistic shape or design.

Serves 10–12

The layered dip is an essential weapon in every Texan's arsenal of party ideas. It works for outdoor pool parties, tailgates, family gatherings, and campfire barbecues. It's an easy dish to take in separate components and build on-site as well, and the garnish on top can be as elaborate as you like. I've seen everything from flags to team logos emblazoned on top of a great layered dip using scallions, tomatoes, black olives and jalapeños. Be creative when you garnish this one, but never let the dip inside be bland!

Green Chile Ratatouille

1 red bell pepper

3 poblano peppers

1 medium onion, diced

4 cloves garlic, peeled and minced

1 small zucchini, diced medium

1 medium eggplant, diced
    medium (about 3 cups)

6 tablespoons extra virgin
    olive oil, divided

3 ounces dry white wine

1 ½ teaspoons kosher salt

2–3 sprigs fresh oregano

3–4 sprigs fresh thyme

6–8 large fresh basil leaves

2 (14-ounce) cans diced tomatoes

1–2 pinches cayenne pepper

Roast the red pepper and poblano peppers over an open flame until well blackened on all sides. Place them in a paper bag or ziplock bag and allow to sweat for 10–15 minutes; then scrape off their skins with the back of a knife blade. Remove the stems and seeds and chop roughly.

In a large sauté pan, cook the onion, garlic, zucchini, eggplant and roasted peppers in half of the olive oil until the onion starts to soften. Deglaze the pan with the white wine, season with salt and cook until the pan is almost dry.

Remove the fresh herbs from their stems and roughly chop. Add the canned tomatoes to the pan along with herbs and cayenne pepper, and simmer lightly together for 7–8 minutes. Drizzle in the remaining olive oil right at the end and stir.

Serves 6–8

 A gas burner works well for roasting the peppers. A gas grill might also get the job done if it has enough power. In a pinch, use the broiler of your oven, but you'll need to lightly coat the peppers in oil first and keep a close eye on them to prevent burning. As a rule, I always watch anything in a broiler without ever turning my back.

Fried Catfish with Smoky Chipotle Tartar Sauce

1 cup buttermilk

1 egg

2 teaspoons hot sauce (I prefer
Crystal brand for this one)

1/2 teaspoon salt

2 cups yellow cornmeal (finely ground
cornmeal, not coarse cornmeal)

1 cup semolina

1 cup corn flour

1 teaspoon salt (not kosher
or large flaked salt)

1 teaspoon ground black pepper

2 teaspoons Texas Red Dirt
Rub Creole Blend

Vegetable oil (enough to fill
your pan 2 inches deep)

6 large catfish fillets,
boneless and skinless

Smoky Chipotle Tartar Sauce

Combine the buttermilk, egg, hot sauce, and salt in a mixing bowl and beat together very well. Combine all dry ingredients in another bowl and mix thoroughly, then scatter out onto a large, flat dinner plate or baking pan.

Pour oil into a deep frying pan and heat to 350 degrees. Dunk each catfish fillet into the wet mix to coat well on all sides, allowing the excess liquid to drain off. Then lay the wet fillets down in the dry mixture; press each fillet down firmly to be sure the coating is equally applied to all sides of the fish. Pan-fry in 350-degree oil for roughly 7 minutes (depending on the size of your fillets), turning over once. The fish should be floating and lightly browned once it's cooked through. Remove to paper towels to drain. Serve immediately with a generous helping of Smoky Chipotle Tartar Sauce.

Serves 6

 The key to making perfect catfish is to get a crispy, light golden-brown crust that has some body to it, a little toothy crunch. This can only be achieved if the fish is cooked in oil that has reached the proper temperature and stays there for the duration of the cooking process. If the oil is too cool, the catfish will be greasy and soggy. If it's too hot, the fish will brown on the outside well before the inside is cooked through. Watch your thermometer closely; fry at 350 degrees and only fry a few fillets at a time with some room in between them and your catfish will come out perfect every time.

SMOKY CHIPOTLE TARTAR SAUCE

3/4 cup mayonnaise

2 chipotle peppers in adobo

1 teaspoon lemon juice

2 teaspoons hot sauce
  (I prefer Crystal Brand)

2 tablespoons chopped
  fresh Italian parsley

1 tablespoon capers, chopped

1 teaspoon Texas Red Dirt
  Rub Creole Blend

Combine the mayo, chipotles, lemon juice, and hot sauce in a blender or food processor and puree until smooth. Remove from the blender and stir in remaining ingredients.

Makes 1 cup

 I use the canned chipotle peppers in adobo sauce for this recipe because they are easy to find, inexpensive, and very flavorful. For most recipes like this, I recommend scraping the seeds out of the peppers before using. They tend to get a little bitter and don't have anything but heat to add. I also tend to use a little extra of the adobo sauce that comes in the can for added smoky flavor.

Angel Hair Pasta with Texas Shrimp and Basil

6 ounces dry angel hair pasta

5 large cloves garlic,
  peeled and minced

3 tablespoons extra virgin
  olive oil, divided

4 large ripe tomatoes,
  cores removed

1 teaspoon salt

1–2 pinches ground black pepper

2/3 cup dry white wine

12 large Texas shrimp,
  peeled and deveined

10 large fresh basil leaves

Cook the pasta in salted boiling water ahead of time; drain and set aside. Most angel hair pasta cooks easily in about 2 minutes, but consult the package on your brand to make sure. It should be cooked "al dente," or just slightly underdone.

In a large sauté pan, cook the garlic in half of the olive oil over medium heat just until it begins to sizzle, then tear the tomatoes apart by hand and add them to the pan. Turn the burner to high, then season the tomatoes with salt and pepper and add in white wine. Allow the sauce to reduce until it begins to thicken slightly (about 4–5 minutes). Add the shrimp and cook for 3–4 minutes, until the shrimp have turned pink and begun to curl. Tear the basil leaves by hand or cut into strips and stir into the sauce. Add the cooked pasta to the sauce and toss a few times to coat. Let the pasta finish cooking for 1 minute in the sauce. Use tongs to transfer the pasta to a large bowl and top with the sauce and shrimp. Drizzle the remaining olive oil on at the last second before serving.

Serves 4

 This dish can be prepared in under 10 minutes and has become one of my favorite go-to meals at home when I'm short on time. The tomatoes can literally be squeezed by hand and torn into pieces to make a quick fresh sauce right in the pan as they cook and give up all of their juices. The success of this dish depends completely on the quality of the tomatoes and shrimp. Use clean, fresh wild shrimp and the ripest tomatoes available, even if they are starting to get a little soft on the outside.

This dish can be served with some additional condiments, such as more chopped cilantro and diced jalapeños. Be sure to find domestic crawfish tails, as they will have tremendously better flavor than the cheaper imported variety. Just because the label might have a Cajun or Texas-sounding name, it still might be from China, so read the fine print. The texture of the crawfish will also be much better when you can find them fresh, but the frozen ones aren't a bad substitute.

Crawfish Enchiladas with Creole Cream Sauce

CREOLE CREAM SAUCE

2 tablespoons butter

2 tablespoons flour

1 yellow onion, diced

4 cloves garlic, peeled and minced

1 red bell pepper, diced

1 green bell pepper, diced

$1/2$ fresh jalapeño

1 rib celery, diced

$1/2$ carrot, peeled and diced

3 tablespoons Texas Red Dirt
      Rub Creole Blend

2 cups chicken stock

2 cups canned chopped tomatoes

1 cup heavy cream

CRAWFISH FILLING

2 tablespoons butter

3 small shallots, minced

1 poblano pepper, seeded and diced

2 pounds crawfish tail meat

1 teaspoon kosher salt

2 Roma tomatoes, seeded and diced

3 tablespoons chopped fresh cilantro

Juice of 1 lime

TORTILLAS

$1/3$ cup vegetable oil for frying

20 corn tortillas

10 ounces queso fresco, grated

For the Creole Cream Sauce: In a large saucepan, melt the butter and add in the flour to from a roux. Stir constantly, cooking the roux over medium-high until it becomes a dark caramel color. Add in the onion, garlic, peppers, celery and carrot and cook for 2 minutes. Season with the Creole Blend, then whisk while adding in the chicken stock to avoid lumps. Add the tomatoes and simmer together for 15 minutes, then puree with a stick blender. Stir in the heavy cream and simmer for an additional 2 minutes.

For the Crawfish Filling: In a large sauté pan, melt the butter and sauté the shallots, pepper and crawfish tails for 3 minutes; season with salt. Add the tomatoes, cilantro, and lime juice, then remove from the heat.

To assemble the enchiladas: In a separate pan, heat the oil and fry the tortillas one at a time for 5–6 seconds on each side just until soft. Drain on paper towels, then fill with the crawfish mixture and roll. Line up the enchiladas in a 9 x 13-inch baking dish. Once the enchiladas are all rolled, pour some of the Creole Cream Sauce over the entire pan, enough to cover the tortillas, and generously sprinkle with grated queso fresco. Bake at 400 degrees for 2–3 minutes, just until the cheese is melted. Serve the enchiladas family style with the remaining sauce on the side.

Serves 10

Chicken and Cactus with Southwestern Romesco

SOUTHWESTERN ROMESCO

3 large tomatoes, cores removed

1 small purple onion, cut
    into thick slices

2 red bell peppers

$1/4$ cup olive oil

$1/3$ cup Spanish almonds

3 cloves garlic, peeled

3 pasilla chiles, stems and
    seeds removed

2 tablespoons red wine vinegar

2 cups chicken stock

2 teaspoons kosher salt

CHICKEN

1 whole chicken, cut into 8 pieces

2 teaspoons kosher salt

Vegetable oil for browning

3 cactus paddles, (often called
    nopales in Mexican markets)

2 yellow onions, diced

1 red bell pepper, diced

To make the sauce, roast the tomatoes, onion slices and red bell peppers over an open flame or grill. Remove the tomatoes and onions when they have become lightly charred on all sides. Roast the peppers until they have completely blackened. Allow the peppers to sweat in a paper bag or ziplock bag for 15 minutes, then remove the skin by scraping it off with the back of a knife. Cut out the stem and seeds.

In a medium saucepan, heat the oil and add in the almonds and garlic cloves just until they begin to brown. Add all remaining ingredients and bring to a simmer. Cover and simmer lightly for 20 minutes. Puree the sauce with a stick blender until smooth.

Season the chicken pieces with salt. Heat the oil in a skillet and brown the chicken on all sides. Drain the pieces on paper towels, then place in a Dutch oven.

Clean the cactus of all needles and slice into strips. Add the cactus strips, onion and diced red pepper to the pot. Pour in the Southwestern Romesco to cover everything. Bring to a simmer on the stovetop, then cover with a tight-fitting lid and simmer on low for 35–40 minutes, or until the chicken is cooked through and tender.

Serves 4–6

This dish is one that I prefer to serve in the center of the table, removing the lid for everyone to see at the last second, sending the steam and complex aromas around the room. It works well served over rice or potatoes and has enough of its own sauce to even require hearty dinner rolls for sopping up the extra. The cactus strips come out so tender and succulent, those who don't know won't even recognize that they are eating cactus.

Red Chili Braised Short Ribs

RED CHILI SAUCE

1 yellow onion, diced

2 ribs celery, diced

5 cloves garlic, peeled and chopped

1 tablespoon butter

3 cascabel chiles

3 guajillo chiles

3 pasilla chiles

1 ancho chile

$2/3$ cup dry red wine

$3^1/2$ cups chicken stock

$1^1/2$ teaspoons kosher salt

$1/2$ teaspoon cracked black pepper

$1/4$ teaspoon ground coriander

$1/2$ teaspoon sweet smoked paprika

1 cinnamon stick

Pinch of ground cumin

2 tablespoons tomato paste

SHORT RIBS

8–10 thick-cut large beef short ribs

1 teaspoon salt

1 tablespoon vegetable oil

$1/2$ cup dry red wine

In a medium-size soup pot, sauté the onion, celery and garlic in butter until the onion softens. Remove the stems and seeds from the dried chiles and add them to the pot. Add the remaining sauce ingredients and cook for 1 hour at a light simmer, covered. Remove the cinnamon stick and puree the entire mixture until smooth, then strain out the solids and discard. Set the sauce aside.

Season the short ribs well with salt. In a Dutch oven, heat the vegetable oil on high heat and brown the short ribs over very high heat on all sides. Once the ribs are very brown, deglaze the pot with red wine, then pour in the Red Chili Sauce and cover with a tight-fitting lid. Place the pot in a preheated 250-degree oven and cook for 5 hours. Once finished, the meat should be fallin'-off-the-bone tender and the sauce incredibly flavorful.

Serves 8–10

 Short ribs are one of the most flavorful cuts in the entire butcher case but require long, slow cooking techniques to make them tender. This is one of those dishes that requires a little work at first, but then it just goes into the oven and comes out perfect every time. I love the rich gravy that forms when the natural juices of the short ribs combine with the earthy chiles to form a complex sauce that begs for a thick slice of bread or a dinner roll for sopping.

Sunday Slow Roast

4 pounds beef chuck roast (or brisket)

2 teaspoons kosher salt

1 teaspoon freshly ground black pepper

2 tablespoons flour

2 tablespoons vegetable oil

1 small yellow onion, diced

3 ribs celery, diced

7 cloves garlic, minced

1 cup dry red wine

1 tablespoon Worcestershire sauce

1 ounce bourbon

1/2 cup black coffee (liquid, no grounds)

2 bay leaves

4–5 sprigs fresh thyme

1 tablespoon tomato paste

FINAL ADDITION

10–12 spring onions or pearl onions

12 baby carrots

1 pound button mushrooms, cleaned

1 pound fingerling potatoes, washed

Pat the roast dry with paper towels and season with salt and pepper on all sides, then dust with the flour. Heat the oil in a large Dutch oven over high heat and brown the roast well on all sides. Add the onion, celery and garlic, then deglaze the pan with red wine. Add all remaining ingredients and cover with a tight-fitting lid. Cook in a preheated oven at 225 degrees for 7–8 hours. Add the final-addition vegetables and cook for 1 more hour.

Serves 10–12

This is the perfect kind of dish to begin on Sunday morning, just before church, and have for dinner that evening. Rich smells and flavors will permeate the whole house all day long.

Those who know me at all know that I just plain don't like coffee. Never have, never will, don't even like the smell of it brewing. But in this particular instance, I find it really adds complexity and flavor to the dish. While the bourbon adds a certain sweetness, the coffee adds earthy and roasty flavors. This dish can even be done in a slow cooker to avoid any mess and cut down on cleanup. If using a slow cooker, begin on high heat for the first 1–2 hours then turn down to low for the rest of the time.

Pork Posole with Dried Chiles

1 1/2 quarts water

4 pounds pork shoulder

1 whole garlic pod,
    divided and peeled

2 tablespoons butter

1 medium sweet onion, diced

2 ribs celery, diced

2 poblano peppers, roasted,
    peeled and seeded

3 quarts chicken stock

5 guajillo chiles, seeds and
    stems removed

3 cascabel chiles, seeds
    and stems removed

Pinch of ground cumin

1/4 teaspoon ground coriander

2 teaspoons Mexican oregano

1 tablespoon kosher salt

1/2 teaspoon pepper

3 (12-ounce) cans white
    hominy, drained

GARNISHES

Freshly diced avocado

Diced radish

Crisp tortilla strips

Fresh cilantro

Lime wedges

In a large stockpot, bring the water and pork to a simmer with all but 3 cloves of the garlic (sliced). Allow the pork and sliced garlic to simmer covered for approximately 1 1/2 hours, or until the pork becomes tender. Remove from the water and discard excess fat and the bone; cut the meat into rough big pieces. Reserve the cooking liquid.

In a separate pot, melt the butter and sauté the onion, remaining garlic (minced), celery and roasted peppers until soft. Add in the chicken stock, dried chiles, cumin, coriander, and oregano and simmer for 40 minutes. Pull out the dried chiles and about 1 cup of the cooking liquid and puree, then return to the pot (it may be necessary to strain out the solids if the chiles don't completely break down when pureed). Once the soup has reached a simmer, add in the pork and about a fourth of the cooking liquid (from the boiled pork). Season with salt and pepper, and add in the hominy. The entire pot of soup should cook together for another 20–30 minutes before serving. Adjust with more liquid if necessary.

Garnish is just as important as the soup when making posole, so be sure to have plenty of nice garnishes to add in at the last minute for each cup.

Serves 10–12

Posole has as many variations as there are cities in Mexico. The only thing they all have in common is rich, hearty, full-flavored soup as the center point of the dish. I love the complex flavors of Mexican oregano with dried chiles, and the contrasting textures of crisp radish with soft avocado—all finished nicely with a crisp, acidic squeeze of lime. Although pork seems more appropriate, chicken or beef certainly could work well in this dish.

Herb-Grilled Shrimp with Cucumber Salad

SHRIMP

2 pounds wild Texas shrimp, 26–30 count
$2/3$ teaspoon Texas Red Dirt
   Rub Creole Blend
15 wooden skewers (or stripped
   rosemary stems)
3 sprigs fresh thyme
3 sprigs fresh dill
3 sprigs fresh oregano
$1/4$ cup extra virgin olive oil

Peel and devein the shrimp, leaving the tails on if you wish. Season lightly with Texas Red Dirt Rub Creole Blend and toss to coat. Soak the skewers or rosemary stems in water for at least 15 minutes to keep them from burning on the grill. Skewer the shrimp, 4 per skewer. Tie the sprigs of fresh herbs together with butcher's twine to form a little herb brush. Dip the brush in the oil and brush some over the grill bars of a hot grill to "season" the bars and help keep the shrimp from sticking. Keep returning the brush to the oil and continue to "season" the bars until the grill is all covered. Grill the shrimp over a hardwood fire (I prefer pecan wood) for approximately 2 minutes per side, or until they are slightly firm and cooked through. Once the shrimp are finished, pile them on top of Cucumber Salad and brush liberally with the now herb-infused olive oil just before eating. Be sure the herb oil never touches the raw shrimp, only the hot grill bars and the cooked shrimp once they are done.

Serves 8

CUCUMBER SALAD

2 large seedless cucumbers
1 Roma tomato, seeded and diced
3 tablespoons chopped fresh chives
1 tablespoon chopped fresh dill
3 tablespoons mayonnaise
Pinch of chipotle chili powder
Pinch of dry mustard powder
Juice and chopped zest of 1 lemon
$1/3$ teaspoon kosher salt
Pinch of celery seed

Peel the cucumbers and cut in half lengthwise, then slice into small half-moon shapes. Mix all remaining ingredients together and dress the cucumbers.

Serves 8

Here's a great summer dish to serve around the pool. The shrimp cook very quickly and can be the centerpiece of conversation for outdoor parties where friends and family gather around the grill to see what the chef is up to. The salad is easy to make ahead of time and bring out on a large platter, just before piling it up with the hot grilled shrimp and taking it to the table. I love to brush the herb-infused oil on at the last minute to give that shine and final touch of flavor to the shrimp.

Creamy Pico de Gallo Shrimp

12 large wild-caught Texas
   shrimp (16–20 count)
2 tablespoons butter
$1/4$ cup diced purple onion
2 cloves garlic, minced
2 fresh jalapeños, seeded and diced
1 ounce dry white wine
1 Roma tomato, seeded and diced
1 tablespoon chopped fresh cilantro
$1/2$ cup heavy cream
Juice of 1 lime
$3/4$ teaspoon kosher salt
Pinch of freshly ground
   black pepper
$1 1/2$ cups cooked white rice

In a hot pan, sear the shrimp in butter for 30 seconds on each side, then remove the shrimp and set aside. In the same pan, sauté the onion, garlic and jalapeños until the onion becomes soft, approximately 3–4 minutes. Deglaze the pan with a splash of dry white wine. Let the wine reduce by half and then add in all remaining ingredients (except the rice), including the partially cooked shrimp. Simmer the contents until the cream has reduced to a slightly thick sauce. Taste for seasonings and plate the entire contents of the pan on a large platter over rice.

Serves 4

 This simple dish can be made in less than 10 minutes and has great flavors that the whole family can enjoy. You can easily adjust the heat by adding or subtracting more jalapeños or more of the seeds if desired. I like to garnish this dish with freshly snipped chives or micro cilantro.

True Texas Chili

4 pounds ground beef chuck*

2 tablespoons Texas Red Dirt
    Rub Southwestern Blend

3 1/2 tablespoons chili powder

1 tablespoon smoked hot paprika

1 teaspoon ground cumin

1 teaspoon ground coriander

Pinch of ground clove

2 teaspoons kosher salt

1 teaspoon cracked black pepper

3 tablespoons canola oil

3 large sweet onions (I prefer
    Texas 1015), diced medium

2 jalapeños, seeded and diced

7 cloves garlic, minced

3 bottles Shiner Bock Beer

1 (6-ounce) can tomato paste

1/2 teaspoon Worcestershire sauce

5–6 dashes hot sauce (I
    prefer Crystal Brand)

3 tablespoons crushed tortilla chips

To the meat, add all dry seasonings and mix well. In a large pot, sear the seasoned meat in canola oil until well browned on all sides. Add the onions, jalapeños, and garlic and cook for 2–3 minutes, stirring often. Add all remaining ingredients and bring to a light simmer. Cover tightly and simmer on low for 2 1/2 hours, then check for consistency: if it's too watery and thin, continue to simmer without the lid until it reduces to a thick consistency. Once the chili has become thick and hearty, it's ready.

Serves 8–10

In Texas, chuck can often be purchased in the form of "chili grind." If not available, buy whole chuck pieces and grind it using the largest plate that your grinder comes with. The grinder attachment for a Kitchen Aide type of mixer is a moderate price and well worth the investment.

In Texas, chili does not have beans. That's not to say that you can't put beans in your chili if you like them, it's just not how real Texas chili is made. Ours is chili con carne, made with meat—lots of it. The quality of the chili is always in direct relation to the quality of the beef you start with and the types of chili powders you use. My favorite source for the best chili powder is Pendery's. They sell online or in person and have more varieties of chili powder than anyone is likely to ever use. Not all chili powders are the same, so be careful what you buy. Anything labeled just chili powder is likely made from whatever pepper happened to be the cheapest on the market on a given day.

King Ranch Casserole

3 cups chicken stock

2 boneless and skinless
  chicken breast halves

4 tablespoons butter, divided

3 tablespoons flour

1 large onion, chopped

4 cloves garlic, minced

2 poblano peppers, chopped

2 ribs celery, chopped

1 teaspoon kosher salt

1/2 teaspoon cracked black pepper

1 teaspoon ancho chili powder

2 Roma tomatoes, seeded and diced

14 corn tortillas

1 pound cheddar cheese, grated

Bring the chicken stock to a simmer and drop in the raw chicken breasts. Simmer lightly for 5–6 minutes, until the chicken is cooked through. Remove the chicken and cut into large chunks to be used later.

In a small pan, cook 3 tablespoons of the butter and flour together while stirring constantly to make a roux. Once the roux begins to lightly brown, remove it from the heat and allow it to cool. Add the roux to the chicken stock while whisking and bring to a boil. (When you add the roux to the stock, either the roux or the stock must be somewhat cool. If both are hot, lumps will form immediately.) Once the stock and roux have come to a boil, the mixture should thicken. Transfer the sauce to a mixing bowl.

In a separate pan, sauté the onion, garlic, peppers, and celery in the remaining butter until they begin to soften. Add the sautéed vegetables to the mixing bowl with the sauce and season with salt, pepper, and chili powder. Add in the diced tomatoes and stir to combine the entire mixture.

Spray a 9 x 13-inch baking dish lightly with olive oil, then tear the tortillas into 2-to-3-inch strips and line the bottom of the dish with a rough layer of torn tortillas. Spoon one-third of the sauce mixture into the dish, followed by one-third of the chicken and one-third of the cheese. Repeat the layers until all ingredients are layered in. The final top layer should be cheese. Bake in a preheated 350-degree oven for 30–35 minutes, until bubbly and the cheese is melted.

Serves 8

Although the King Ranch in south Texas serves this dish to guests, the casserole did not originate there, nor does anyone know for sure how it got this name. Regardless of the true history, this enchilada-like casserole is a family favorite across the Lone Star State, popular with kids and adults alike. Many recipes call for cream of this or that soup, but for true Texas flavor, it's better to start with fresh ingredients.

Pecan-Smoked Spicy Chicken

2 cups water

2 1/2 teaspoons cayenne pepper

1 teaspoon garlic powder

1 1/2 tablespoons salt

1 tablespoon honey

1 whole all-natural chicken,
   roughly 5–5 1/2 pounds

2 tablespoons Texas Red Dirt
   Rub Southwestern Blend

Combine the water, pepper, garlic powder, salt, and honey in a pot and heat over the stove until completely dissolved together; let cool in the fridge.

Place the chicken in a 2-gallon ziplock freezer bag and pour in the brine. Force out as much air as possible then seal the bag. Allow the chicken to soak in the refrigerator overnight, turning several times to ensure the brine reaches the entire bird. Remove the chicken from the bag the following day, drain off all of the brine and pat the bird dry with paper towels. Rub the bird well with the Southwestern Blend, even the inside of the cavity. Truss the bird with kitchen twine, pulling the legs and wings in tight to ensure it cooks evenly. Place the bird in a smoker with pecan chips and cook at 250 degrees until done, about 2 hours. Gas grill alternative: Turn one burner on high and leave one burner off. Place a foil package of pecan wood chips over the hot side until they begin to smoke. Place the bird on the cool side, pull down the lid and allow to smoke. Turn the bird once in a while to ensure even cooking, and refresh the chips as needed to maintain a smoky environment inside your gas grill.

Serves 4

 A perfectly roasted chicken is every chef's baseline for home-cooked meals, but I simply love to use my smoker. This makes an incredibly juicy and full-flavored bird that is tasty on its own but can also be the perfect base for many other dishes, like smoked chicken salad or enchiladas. I strongly recommend using an accurate kitchen thermometer for this recipe. Two hours is usually sufficient to cook a 5 1/2-pound chicken, but smokers and grills can greatly vary. I prefer a thermometer that has a cord attached so I can watch the internal temp climb as the bird is cooking. Pull the bird when the deepest part of the chicken registers 160 degrees.

Green Chile Chilaquiles

2 fresh jalapeños (seeds optional)

1 small purple onion

Juice of 2 limes

2 pinches kosher salt

5 ounces corn tortilla chips

1 1/2 cups shredded cooked chicken

3 cups Roasted Salsa Verde
  (see page 14)

1 cup queso fresco, grated

GARNISHES:

1/2 cup sour cream

1 bunch fresh cilantro, chopped

1 ripe avocado, sliced

Slice the jalapeños and onion into thin julienne strips. Mix both with lime juice and salt and let marinate together for 1 hour.

Arrange the corn chips randomly in a large casserole dish, then top with shredded chicken. Warm the salsa in a pan and pour over the chips and chicken. Top with queso fresco and bake at 350 degrees for 10–12 minutes, just until the cheese has melted and the casserole is hot. Remove from the oven and garnish the top with the pickled jalapeño and onion strips, plenty of sour cream, fresh cilantro, and avocado slices. Another option is to serve the cold garnishes on the side.

Serves 6

 Chilaquiles is the dish that eventually led to what we now call nachos. It's sort of a spicy Mexican casserole, bursting with flavor—true comfort food in Texas. The other option for this dish is to put all of the components out like a buffet and allow each person to build their bowl with chips, chicken, cheese, etc., then ladle over the hot salsa.

Pecan-Stuffed Pork Chops

1 large rack of pork chops, bones in
4 tablespoons butter
$1/2$ yellow onion, chopped
2 ribs celery, chopped
5 cloves garlic, minced
$1 1/2$ cups chicken stock
1 teaspoon kosher salt
$1/4$ teaspoon cayenne pepper
2 cups panko bread crumbs
2 cups Sweet 'n' Hot Roasted
    Pecans (See page 82), chopped
More kosher salt and
    pepper to taste

Clean the rack of pork well and cut in between the bones to get thick individual pork chops. Cut a large slit down the back side of each chop and insert the tip of a knife 2–3 inches inside the chop to create a pocket for the stuffing. Do not poke completely through the pork or the stuffing will not stay in.

In a large saucepan, melt the butter and sauté the onion, celery, and garlic until the onion has slightly softened. Add the chicken stock, salt, and cayenne and bring to a light simmer. Pour the contents into a mixing bowl and add the panko bread crumbs and pecans. Mix together and let cool to room temperature. Stuff as much of the mixture into each pork chop as will fit (overstuffing is okay, too). Sprinkle both sides of each chop with salt and pepper to taste, then roast in a preheated 400-degree oven for 12 minutes. Turn the chops over once and roast an additional 15 minutes. Check for doneness with a meat thermometer; I prefer pork cooked to 135–140 degrees (or medium).

Serves 7–8

 These overstuffed chops are a great dish to serve family style and need very little accompaniment, as they are already bursting with starch. They pair well with simple sautéed spinach or southern-style greens. I especially like the way the stuffing absorbs any extra juices from the pork and delivers a meal almost in itself.

The Texas coastline is bursting with fresh seafood, and this sandwich combines three of my all-time favorites. This is exactly the kind of dish I like to prepare for casual parties based around sporting events. Guys love the big whole sandwiches, but most ladies prefer to cut them into smaller sizes, with a toothpick in the center to hold the smaller versions together. Either way, it's a seafood indulgence with just enough spice to make this dish a huge hit with almost any crowd.

Oyster, Shrimp, and Crawfish PoBoys with Jalapeño Remoulade

SEAFOOD FILLING

1/2 pound crawfish tails
1/2 pound gulf shrimp (26–30 count), peeled and deveined
1/2 pound gulf oysters, freshly shucked
1 1/2 cups buttermilk
2 tablespoons hot sauce
1 cup flour
1 cup corn flour
1/4 cup cornmeal
1 tablespoon Texas Red Dirt Rub Creole Blend
Oil for deep-frying
Jalapeño Remoulade
1 head iceberg lettuce, shredded
3 ripe tomatoes, sliced
4–6 large PoBoy sandwich rolls

To prepare the seafood filling, combine all of the seafood with buttermilk and hot sauce and allow to marinate for 15–20 minutes in the fridge. Place flour, corn flour and Creole Blend in a large mixing bowl and whisk to combine.

To deep-fry the seafood in batches, pull the seafood mixture out of the liquid a small handful at a time, allowing the excess juices to drain off; add the seafood to the dry ingredients. Toss by hand until each piece is well coated on all sides. Deep-fry the seafood in 350-degree oil, turning occasionally, until golden brown and crisp. This should take about 2 minutes per batch. Drain the seafood immediately on paper towels. Assemble each sandwich with plenty of remoulade, shredded cool lettuce, and sliced tomato on PoBoy rolls.

Serves 4–6

JALAPEÑO REMOULADE

2 fresh jalapeños, seeded and diced
2 tablespoons chopped Italian parsley
1 tablespoon capers, chopped
1 teaspoon lemon juice
2 teaspoons hot sauce
3/4 cup mayonnaise
Pinch of hot smoked paprika
1 teaspoon Texas Red Dirt Rub Creole Blend

Combine all ingredients and mix well.

Fort Worth Fancy

I use the term "Fort Worth Fancy" at my restaurant to describe everything from the cuisine to our dress code.

When potential patrons ask how to dress, my reply is, "It's only Fort Worth Fancy." That's our way of telling customers to be as comfortable as they like while still giving the impression of an upscale place.

My hometown is Fort Worth. It's known for great food and lack of pretense, but it's not unsophisticated. We appreciate boldness around here, never having to apologize for skimpy portions or bland tastes. When it's time to throw a dinner party in this town, folks have a way of trying to outdo each other in a good-natured kind of way. Fort Worth Fancy is our way of being dressed up but not over the top, and cooking great meals that don't have any of that big city over-sophistication with too many microscopic ingredients or overly difficult plating presentations. We celebrate our local ingredients and flavors and cook fancy when the time is right. Here are a few dishes to help make your next dinner party a bigger success.

Avocado, Shrimp, and Crab Salad with Tarragon Mustard Vinaigrette

2 large ripe avocados, diced
$1/2$ pound baby shrimp, cooked
$1/2$ pound lump crabmeat, picked
   through for shell pieces
2 tablespoons freshly chopped chives
Juice of 1 lemon
$1 1/2$ teaspoons extra virgin olive oil
$1/4$ teaspoon kosher salt
Pinch of white pepper

Place a 4-inch ring mold in the center of a chilled salad plate and fill 1 inch high with diced avocado. In a bowl, combine the seafood and dress with all remaining ingredients. Toss lightly, being careful not to break up the pieces of crab. Add a few spoonfuls of the seafood mixture on top of the avocado and press lightly on top with the back of a spoon to pack it down. Remove the ring mold and then drizzle the vinaigrette over the top to finish the dish.

Serves 6–7

TARRAGON MUSTARD VINAIGRETTE

Juice of 1 lemon
2 teaspoons white wine vinegar
6 teaspoons extra virgin olive oil
3–4 sprigs fresh tarragon,
   leaves chopped
1 teaspoon Dijon mustard
$1/4$ teaspoon kosher salt
Pinch of freshly ground black pepper

Whisk all ingredients together well and drizzle over the prepared salad.

I love this dish for its simplicity and the way it highlights beautiful ingredients without overwhelming them. Avocado and crab are my two favorite ingredients, and topping them with just the right blend of fresh tarragon with enough acidic bite to accent (but not overpower) the dish is a thing of beauty. The presentation is really simple as well, but elegant in a way. Simply using a ring mold (or a cut ring of PVC pipe) to arrange the avocado and crab in a perfect circle makes each dish look spectacular and shows off the gorgeous colors.

Butternut Squash Soup with Chile Spiced Pumpkin Seeds

1 large butternut squash
1 large yellow onion, chopped
3 cloves garlic, chopped
2 tablespoons butter
2 tablespoons olive oil
2 teaspoons kosher salt
2 ounces dry white wine
1 star anise
1 cinnamon stick
4 cups chicken or vegetable stock
1 cup heavy cream
Juice of 2 oranges
Sweet Heat Pumpkin Seeds*
    (see page 195)

Peel the squash with a sharp knife and split in half lengthwise. Scrape out the seeds and stringy membranes and then dice into large cubes; set aside. In a large soup pot, lightly sweat the onion and garlic in butter and olive oil until soft. Add the squash and season with salt. Deglaze the pan with white wine and simmer for 1 minute. Add all remaining ingredients, except pumpkin seeds, and bring to a simmer. Simmer covered for 25–30 minutes. Discard the cinnamon stick and star anise; puree the entire mixture with a stick blender. Serve the soup with a sprinkle of chile-spiced Sweet Heat Pumpkin Seeds on top.

Serves 6

This is a wonderful dish to serve in the fall when butternut squash becomes abundant. The sweetness of the squash contrasts well with the texture and light spice of the pepitas. The seeds of the squash can also be washed and used instead of pepitas, but they can be somewhat inconsistent from one squash to another. Try them simply roasted with salt and a touch of olive oil as a great snack.

Seared Avocado with Shellfish Salad

1 poblano pepper
1 ear fresh corn, husked
8 ounces bay scallops, cleaned
8 ounces lump crabmeat
$1/8$ teaspoon turmeric
Pinch of chiles de arbol
Pinch of smoked paprika
Pinch of garlic powder
1 teaspoon canola oil
$1/2$ cup medium-diced celery
3 tablespoons chopped fresh chives
2 tablespoons mayonnaise
Juice of 1 lemon
3 ripe avocados
Salt and black pepper to taste

For the salad: Roast the poblano over an open flame until black on all sides, then allow to sweat in a bag for 10–15 minutes, or until cool enough to handle. Scrape off the black skin with the back edge of a knife, remove the seeds and stem, and dice. Roast corn over an open flame or grill until the kernels are golden brown or lightly charred; cut corn from the cob and set aside.

Place scallops and crabmeat in a bowl. Combine all of the dry seasonings and add them to the seafood mixture; toss to coat.

Allow the seafood to soak in the seasonings for 10–15 minutes in the fridge.

To a very hot cast-iron skillet, add a drizzle of canola oil, then sear the scallops and crab very quickly. Turn often and let cook until done. This should usually take about 2–3 minutes, depending on the size of the scallops. Remember not to overcrowd the pan. If the pan cannot handle all of the seafood at once, cook in several batches. Cool the seafood in the fridge before proceeding.

In a mixing bowl, combine the seafood with celery, chives, mayonnaise and lemon juice. Taste for seasonings. The heat level can be adjusted by adding more chiles de arbol if necessary.

For the avocado: Cut the avocados in half, remove the seeds, and scoop each half from the skin with a spoon. Season the avocados with salt and pepper on all sides, then sear in a hot nonstick skillet with just a touch of oil until browned on both sides. It will help if you cut a flat spot on the curved side to allow the avocado to have two flat sides to brown.

Once the avocados are browned, place each one on a plate with the hole facing up. Fill with heaping spoonfuls of the seafood salad.

Makes 6 large portions

 I've always considered the avocado to be my true favorite food. I was so intrigued—if not slightly alarmed—when I saw a menu featuring seared avocado that I had to order it just to see what this was all about. I was pleasantly surprised to find that getting a nice brown sear on the outside of an avocado turned the already stellar fruit into something more complex and flavorful than I imagined. I don't recommend actually cooking the avocado in this dish, just searing it to get a nice caramelized layer on the outside. Topping this off with a spicy chilled seafood salad makes this a perfect dish for friends or family on special occasions.

Creole Roasted Turkey with Southwestern Sage Gravy

1 1/2 gallons water

1 1/2 cups honey

2 cups kosher salt

2 cups orange juice

1 (12-pound) fresh turkey

1/2 cup brown sugar

1/2 cup Texas Red Dirt
Rub Creole Blend

Warm the water slightly and add the honey, salt, and orange juice. Stir until the honey and salt have completely dissolved, then cool the water down (ice works well) and submerge the turkey in the brine overnight. The brining turkey needs to stay at refrigerated temperature.

Clean and rinse the turkey thoroughly and pat dry with paper towels. Combine the sugar and Texas Red Dirt Rub, then liberally season the entire turkey, even inside the cavity. Truss the bird with kitchen twine by tying the legs and wings in tight so that the bird cooks evenly. Roast the turkey in a 385-degree convection oven for the first 40 minutes. (If using a non-convection oven, start at 400 degrees, then turn down to 300. It may take longer to cook.) Turn down the oven to 300 degrees and cook until the internal temperature reaches 155 degrees on a meat thermometer. This should take approximately 2 to 2 1/2 hours, but ovens will vary.

Serves 8

 Do not be alarmed when this turkey gets a really dark mahogany color on the outside. The sugar will caramelize and get darker than most people are used to seeing. If the bird gets too dark, lightly cover with a tent of foil to protect the exterior of the bird from burning. Depending on the type of roasting pan you are using, sometimes adding a little water to the bottom of the pan helps keep the oven environment nice and moist while the bird cooks.

SOUTHWESTERN SAGE GRAVY

2 tablespoons butter

2 tablespoons flour

2 tablespoons minced shallots

2 cloves garlic, minced

2 cups pan drippings (supplement
   with chicken stock if needed)

3/4 cup heavy cream

2 tablespoons chopped fresh sage

1 teaspoon kosher salt

1/4 teaspoon white pepper

1/2 teaspoon ground coriander

In a heavy-bottomed skillet, melt the butter, then stir in
the flour over low-to-medium heat to make a roux. Do
not stop stirring once the mixture is combined. Cook
until the roux becomes bubbly and starts to smell like
sourdough toast, but do not allow it to become dark
brown. Add in the shallots and garlic and stir while
cooking for 1–2 minutes, then add in the pan drippings
(and/or chicken stock). Whisk until the mixture comes
to a simmer. You will not see any thickening until the
liquid simmers. Once the gravy thickens, add in the
cream, sage and seasonings, and simmer lightly for 3–4
minutes. Taste for the right amount of salt and pepper.
Serve hot.

Serves 8

Crab and Red Pepper Bisque with Pecans

3 red bell peppers
1 large sweet onion, chopped
4 cloves garlic, minced
1 tablespoon butter
1 1/2 teaspoons kosher salt
2 pinches ground white pepper
1/2 cup dry white wine
2 cups heavy cream
Juice of 1 lime

CRAB

6 ounces lump crabmeat
1/2 teaspoon extra virgin olive oil
1/2 lime, juice only
Pinch of kosher salt
1/4 cup Sweet 'n' Hot
    Roasted Pecans, roughly
    chopped (see page 82)

Roast the red peppers over an open flame until black on all sides. Allow them to sweat in a paper bag or ziplock bag for 10–15 minutes, or until cool enough to handle. Scrape off the skins with the back of a knife blade and remove the stem and seeds. Sauté the onion and garlic in butter until the onions soften, then add in the roasted peppers. Season with salt and white pepper then deglaze the pan with white wine. Reduce by half. Add the cream and lime juice and simmer for 3–4 minutes. Puree with a stick blender until smooth.

Toss the crab with the oil and lime juice and season lightly with salt. Place a little of the crab mixture in each serving cup or bowl, then pour the hot soup over and top with pecans.

Serves 4–6

 This dish is the perfect balance between sweet pecans and crab, brought together with the slightly bitter note of red pepper, earthy roasted undertones, and a crisp acidic finish of lime. The wonderful mélange of textures, flavors and stunning red color is sure to impress at any gathering.

Jalapeño Lime Mussels

1 pound live mussels (I love
the PEI variety)

2 cloves garlic, minced

1 large jalapeño, seeded and diced

1 tablespoon butter

1 ounce dry white wine

1 ounce heavy cream

1 Roma tomato, seeded and diced

Juice of 1 lime

1 teaspoon fresh cilantro, chopped

1/4 teaspoon kosher salt

Clean the mussels one at a time by rinsing and pulling off any "beard" that might be attached. (The beard is nothing more than the part of the mussel that attaches itself to the ropes that PEI mussels are grown on. Sometimes they still have a small piece of that rope attached.) In a medium-size pot, sauté the garlic and jalapeño in butter for 1 minute. Add the white wine and cream and bring to a simmer. Add all remaining ingredients, stir once, and cover with a lid. Simmer for 2 minutes, or until all mussels have opened. Serve immediately with a rustic bread for sopping up the extra sauce.

Serves 2

 Mussels are one of the easiest seafood items to cook at home and should not be thought of as intimidating. They simply need to be cooked with some great flavors, and once they have all opened up, the dish is done. If any mussel in the pot does not open after all of the others have, pull that one out and discard it. This dish works equally as well with clams.

Scallops with Orange and Sage Butter

6 large diver scallops (dry-
   packed, U10 size)

$^1/_4$ teaspoon kosher salt

1 teaspoon olive oil

1 clove garlic, minced

1 ounce dry white wine

Juice of 1 orange

4–5 large fresh sage leaves, chopped

4 tablespoons butter

Wash the scallops and remove the small muscle sometimes attached to the side. Pat dry with a paper towel, then season lightly with salt on both sides. Add the oil to a very hot nonstick or cast-iron pan and sear the scallops on each side until they are well browned. Remove the scallops from the pan and set aside once they are cooked through. If they need further cooking, depending on the thickness of the scallops, finish the cooking for a few minutes in a 350-degree oven. Quickly sauté the garlic in the scallop pan, then deglaze with the wine. Reduce until the pan is almost dry. Add the orange juice and the sage and cook to reduce by half. Add the butter and swirl the pan until the butter is fully incorporated. Check the level of salt and immediately pour the sauce over the scallops.

Serves 2–3

 Be sure to buy scallops for this dish that are dry-packed (as opposed to wet-packed). Dry-packed scallops tend to be fresher and will brown up very nicely with a caramelized sear. Wet-packed scallops have been treated to make them last longer, and it's very difficult to get them to brown. Your fishmonger should know the difference.

Chili-Crusted Scallops with Anaheim Chile–Lime Sauce

12 large diver scallops
2 teaspoons kosher salt
1/2 teaspoon ground black pepper
2 teaspoons dark chili powder (I prefer
    Pendery's Durango blend for this one)
4 tablespoons clarified butter
Grits, rice, or potatoes

Clean the scallops well, detach the little side muscle if it's on there, and pat dry with paper towels. Mix the salt, pepper and chili powder and coat the scallops well on all sides. Let the scallops soak in the dry spice for about 5 minutes before cooking. Cook the scallops in a hot nonstick pan with clarified butter. Allow them to really sizzle on each side and brown before turning. Depending on the size of scallops, it should take about 2 minutes per side to sear to medium rare. If they are particularly large, they may require additional cooking in the oven to finish. Place the scallops over grits, rice or your favorite potatoes and top with Anaheim Chili–Lime Sauce.

Serves 4–6

ANAHEIM CHILE–LIME SAUCE

1 small sweet onion, diced
3 cloves garlic, minced
1 teaspoon olive oil
10 dried red Anaheim chiles,
    stems and seeds removed
2 1/2 cups chicken stock
1/3 cup canned diced tomatoes
2 ounces white wine
1 teaspoon kosher salt
Juice of 2 limes

In a medium-size saucepan, sweat the onion and garlic in oil until soft. Add all remaining ingredients except the lime juice and bring to a simmer. Simmer covered for 30 minutes. Puree with a stick blender and strain. Add the lime juice at the end and serve.

Makes 3 cups

 This method of putting a little chili powder on the outside of the scallops before cooking develops an incredibly rich outer coating once the scallops have been seared and really works well with the tangy and rich Anaheim sauce. Don't be afraid to pour a little extra sauce for sopping up with grits or your favorite starch.

Green Chile and Oyster Dressing

4–5 slices day old bread (a
  rich, hearty bread like
  challah works best)
4 poblano peppers
2 tablespoons olive oil
1 small onion, chopped
2 ribs celery, chopped
5 cloves garlic, minced
1 1/2 tablespoons Texas Red
  Dirt Rub Creole Blend
2 teaspoons dried sage
2 teaspoons dried parsley
1/2 teaspoon freshly ground pepper
2 cups chicken stock
1 1/2 cups clam juice
2 dozen Texas oysters,
  freshly shucked
1 cup panko bread crumbs

Dry the slices of bread in a 250-degree oven until crisp but not browned. Cut into cubes and set aside. Roast the poblanos over a flame until blackened on all sides. Allow to sweat in a paper bag or ziplock bag for 10–15 minutes, then scrape off the skins with the back of a knife blade. Remove and discard the stems and seeds; chop. Heat olive oil in a skillet and sauté the onion, roasted chiles, celery, and garlic until soft. Season with all dry seasonings, then add in the chicken stock and clam juice; bring the mixture to a light simmer. Add in the fresh oysters and simmer for 3–4 minutes. Add the panko bread crumbs and dried bread cubes; combine and serve.

Serves 8–10

There are so many different ways to make the traditional dressing that accompanies roasted turkey, and each one has its merit, but this particular dressing is my all-time favorite. It has just enough spice to be flavorful but not enough to hurt anybody, and the slightly salty oysters are my favorite bites in the dish. I do not recommend stuffing this type of dressing (or any for that matter) inside a turkey when it cooks. Turkey will roast better without any filling whatsoever.

Classic Shrimp Cocktail with Sauces

FOR THE SHRIMP:

2 pounds wild-caught whole gulf
   shrimp, 16–20 count (I prefer
   the white shrimp for this recipe)

2 gallons water

10–15 black peppercorns

2 bay leaves

3 tablespoons kosher salt

2 oranges, halved

2 lemons, halved

1 teaspoon garlic powder

1 teaspoon onion powder

1 recipe Jalapeño Remoulade
   (see page 85)

1 recipe Chipotle Cocktail
   Sauce (see page 105)

In a large pot, bring all ingredients, except sauces, to a boil for 4 full minutes. Drop in the shrimp and cook until the water comes back to a full rolling boil; cook for 1 full minute. This should be enough to cook the shrimp all the way through. Remove the shrimp and plunge them into ice water to stop the cooking process. Test one by cutting in half to ensure they are cooked through. Remove the heads and peel the shrimp, leaving the tail shell on, and remove any vein along the back. This can easily be done with the tines of a dinner fork or using a specialized shrimp deveiner and peeler, sold in many stores. Serve chilled with two sauces.

Serves 6–8

Texas is one of the leading shrimp-producing states in the nation, both in wild-caught shrimp and aqua-cultured varieties. I cook with shrimp so often and in so many ways that I sometimes need to just get back to basics and enjoy shrimp in its pure form. I love simple boiled shrimp, with just enough flavor to enhance but not overpower the delicate and sweet original taste. Both of these dipping sauces are real crowd pleasers as well. Be generous when planning for how much shrimp to make for a party. As any restaurateur can tell you, shrimp is the most voraciously attacked item on any buffet.

CHIPOTLE COCKTAIL SAUCE

3/4 cup drained, diced
   canned tomatoes
3/4 cup ketchup
3 tablespoons prepared horseradish
1 dash Worcestershire sauce
1 chipotle pepper (with 1/2 teaspoon
   of the adobo sauce from the can)
Juice of 1 lemon
1/2 teaspoon kosher salt
Pinch of ground black pepper

Mix all ingredients using a food processor until smooth.

Makes 1 3/4 cups

Chicken Fried Tenderloin Sliders with Jalapeño and Bacon Cream Gravy

1 1/2 pounds beef tenderloin
1 cup buttermilk
Salt
Cracked pepper to taste
1/2 cup flour
Canola oil for frying
10 slider rolls
1 jalapeño pepper, thinly sliced

Cut the tenderloin into roughly 2-ounce thin medallions. Place in a bowl and cover with the buttermilk and season lightly with salt. Let sit for 5 minutes. Season flour well with salt and pepper. Pull the steaks out of the buttermilk and heavily coat each one with seasoned flour. Heat oil in a large skillet and pan-fry the steaks on both sides just until lightly browned. Remove and drain on paper towels. Serve immediately on rolls topped with Jalapeño and Bacon Cream Gravy and an extra slice of jalapeño.

Makes 10 small sliders

JALAPEÑO AND BACON CREAM GRAVY

2 strips bacon, diced
1 tablespoon butter
1 jalapeño, diced
2 tablespoons minced shallot
1 tablespoon flour
1 1/2 cups half-and-half
1/2 teaspoon kosher salt
Pinch cracked black pepper

Begin by rendering the bacon in a large pan. When the bacon has mostly rendered but is not yet crispy, add in the butter, jalapeño, and shallot. Sauté for one minute, then sprinkle in the flour and whisk. Cook until the flour begins to just lightly brown, then add in the half-and-half. Whisk quickly to combine, and continue whisking until the gravy reaches a simmer. Season with salt and pepper; simmer until the gravy reaches the perfect thickness. If it comes out too thin, keep reducing until it thickens. If too thick, add a touch more half-and-half to thin it out.

Makes 1 3/4 cups

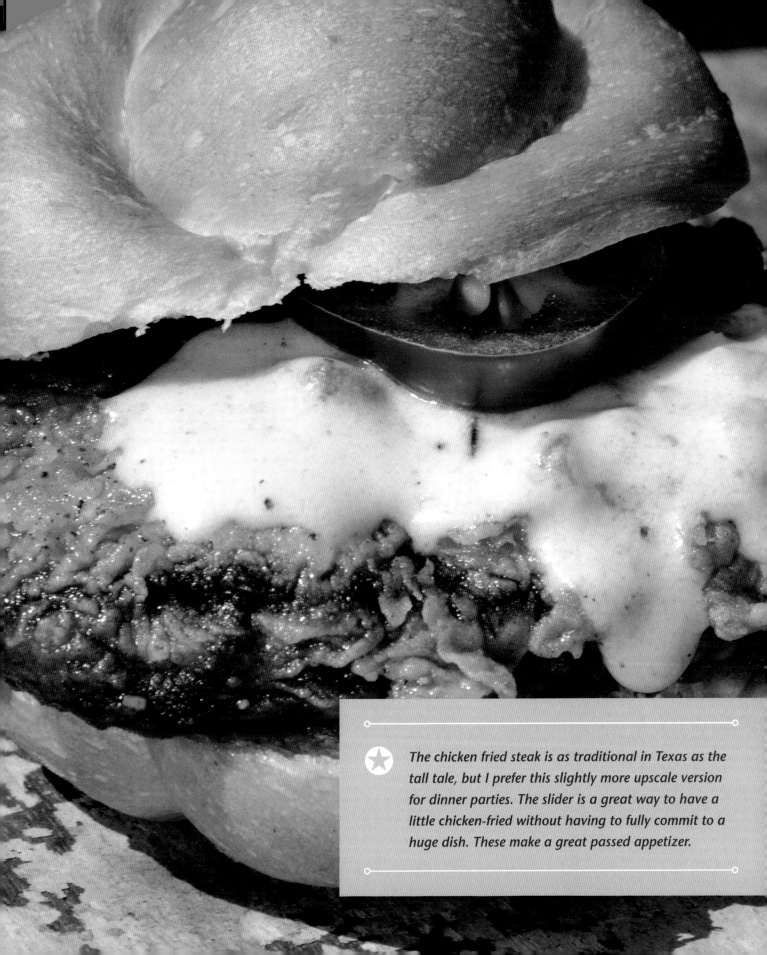

The chicken fried steak is as traditional in Texas as the tall tale, but I prefer this slightly more upscale version for dinner parties. The slider is a great way to have a little chicken-fried without having to fully commit to a huge dish. These make a great passed appetizer.

Smoked Tenderloin with Southwestern Skillet Potatoes

1 whole beef tenderloin
(approximately 5 pounds)
$^1/_4$ cup Texas Red Dirt
Rub Creole Blend
1 recipe Southwestern Skillet
Potatoes (see page 192)

Rub the beef on all sides with the seasoning mix and let sit for 1 hour at room temperature to soak in. Place in a smoker loaded with pecan wood chips and cook until the internal temperature reaches 128 degrees. If using a gas grill, turn one burner on high and leave one burner off. Place a foil package of pecan wood chips over the hot side until they begin to smoke. Place the beef on the cool side, pull down the lid and allow to smoke. Turn the beef once in a while to ensure even cooking, and refresh the chips as needed to maintain a smoky environment inside your gas grill. Let meat rest for 5–7 minutes before slicing, then serve over Southwestern Skillet Potatoes.

Serves 12

This is a large-platter type of meal that begs to be served family style, right in the center of the table; yet it's luxurious enough for a dinner party as well. The beef can be sliced thin for larger groups (and makes for great sandwiches if there are leftovers), or thicker for larger appetites, if you prefer. Tenderloin takes on smoke flavors extremely well, and this dish is one of the richest ways to enjoy such a decadent cut of meat.

Roasted Poblano, Crab, and Corn Soup

3 poblano peppers

2 ears fresh corn, husked

1 large sweet onion, chopped

4 cloves garlic, minced

1 tablespoon butter

1 1/2 teaspoons kosher salt

1/4 teaspoon white pepper

4 ounces dry white wine

1 1/2 cups heavy cream

1 1/2 cups chicken stock

1/2 pound fresh crab claw meat (or lump meat), picked through for shell pieces

Juice of 1 lime

Roast the poblanos over a flame until blackened on all sides. Allow to sweat in a paper bag or ziplock bag for 10–15 minutes, then scrape off the skins with the back of a knife blade. Remove the stem and seeds and chop the peppers. Grill the corn ears until they have lightly browned on all sides; remove corn from the cob with a chef's knife.

In a large soup pot, sweat the onion, garlic, and half of the roasted peppers in butter. Once the vegetables have softened, season with salt and pepper, then add in the white wine. Reduce the wine by three-fourths, and then add in the cream and stock. Bring to a simmer and puree with a stick blender until smooth. Add in the crabmeat, corn, remaining roasted peppers, and lime juice and simmer for 1 minute. Stir gently and serve.

Serves 4–6

This is a great dish to serve in early spring when the water in the Gulf begins to warm up and the crabs become active. Great fresh crabmeat is the key to making this dish successful.

Green Chile and Cheese-Stuffed Okra

15 pieces fresh okra, the
    longer the better
2 fresh Hatch green chiles
$1/2$ cup finely shredded
    cheddar cheese
1 egg yolk
1 clove garlic, minced
Pinch smoked hot paprika
$1/4$ teaspoon kosher salt
Pinch of cayenne pepper

BEER BATTER
1 cup flour
1 egg yolk
1 teaspoon sugar
$1/2$ teaspoon kosher salt
Pinch of cayenne pepper
1 cup Shiner Bock Beer

Cut the okra lengthwise in half and scrape out most of the seeds to form a long pocket inside. Roast the chiles over a flame until blackened on all sides. Allow to sweat in a paper bag or ziplock bag for 10–15 minutes, then scrape off the skins with the back of a knife blade. Remove and discard the stem and seeds; chop. Combine the chiles with the cheese, egg yolk, garlic, and seasonings. Stuff the okra and pack very tightly with the cheese mixture, then allow to cool in the fridge for 20 minutes.

Combine the Beer Batter ingredients, except the beer, in a mixing bowl and whisk together well. Slowly add in the beer while whisking and stir until a uniform batter is formed.

Dip the chilled and stuffed okra into the batter, coating each one well, then fry in 365-degree oil for 2–3 minutes, until golden brown all over. Turn the okra often to ensure all sides brown evenly. Drain on paper towels and serve hot.

Serves 5–6

 When Hatch green chiles come in season at the end of the summer, they make the perfect pepper for this dish, with just the right amount of heat and intense flavor. When they aren't available, Anaheim or jalapeño peppers will do, but I prefer the Hatch. Even those who claim they don't like okra will have a hard time passing up these flavor-packed morsels.

Cooking Outdoors

My favorite place to cook anything is still in the great outdoors. Give me a grill, a smoker, or even an open fire pit and my mind immediately goes back to my childhood and cooking with my father. Momma cooked in the kitchen, but Dad ruled the grill when it came to cooking at the Bonnell household. Dad took a seat-of-your-pants approach to cooking, never being one to enjoy following recipes.

Texas outdoor cooking generally revolves around big, bold proteins but can take a few creative turns once in a while. When we think of barbecue, it's beef brisket and pork ribs, both with loads of smoke flavor. The sauce is thick, sweet, usually smoky and always tangy, with spice optional. I can usually judge an outdoor cook in about five minutes by just watching him man the grill or smoker. It's easy to spot the guy or gal who's been around the block a few times and knows the right moves, the right equipment and the right techniques. The rookie is also easy to spot, with too many non-essential gimmicky gadgets and a tendency to flip everything on the grill at least ten times before it's finished.

This chapter includes something for every outdoor occasion, whether you are trying to feed the masses from a smoke pit or entertaining around the pool for an upscale gathering.

Grilled Summer Vegetable Salad with Southwestern Buttermilk Dressing

2 zucchini

2 yellow summer squash

2 portabella mushrooms

2 red bell peppers

1 small purple onion

1 eggplant

1 bunch asparagus

10–12 baby carrots

1 bunch scallions

1 tablespoon kosher salt

1/2 tablespoon freshly
    ground black pepper

1/2 teaspoon garlic powder

3 tablespoons olive oil

Cut all vegetables into large, thick slices (except for asparagus, carrots and scallions, which can be left whole) and place in a large mixing bowl. Sprinkle with salt, pepper and garlic powder and drizzle with olive oil. Toss to coat the veggies well, then grill all of them over a hardwood grill. I prefer pecan or mesquite wood, but hickory, apple and cherry all have great flavors as well. When tender, arrange the vegetables on a platter and serve with Southwestern Buttermilk Dressing on the side for dipping.

Serves 6–8

 This may be the only ranch-type dressing you'll ever find that uses all natural ingredients with no MSG. Monosodium glutamate is a chemical food enhancer that I try to avoid. I prefer naturally bold flavors without additives. For these types of platters, I love to wander around our local farmers market and see what catches my eye. It always helps to bring a range of colors and textures to the table—variety for the palate.

SOUTHWESTERN BUTTERMILK DRESSING:

$^1/_2$ cup buttermilk

$^1/_2$ cup mayonnaise

2 tablespoons sour cream

1 teaspoon dried parsley flakes

$^1/_2$ teaspoon freshly ground
   black pepper

1 teaspoon garlic powder

$^1/_2$ teaspoon chopped fresh chives

$^1/_2$ teaspoon onion powder

$^1/_4$ teaspoon dried thyme

Pinch of cayenne pepper

2 teaspoons Texas Red Dirt
   Rub Creole Blend

4–5 shakes hot sauce

Combine all ingredients and whisk briskly. Let sit for at least 30 minutes before serving.

Makes 1$^1/_4$ cups

Grilled Striper with Cactus and Black Beans

4 fillets wild striped bass,
approximately 8 ounces each*

1 teaspoon Texas Red Dirt Rub
Southwestern Blend

1 tablespoon canola oil

4 cactus paddles**

3 cups Bacon-Laced Black
Beans (see page 185)

1 lemon

*Texas farm-raised bass is a great
substitute.*

**Called nopales in Mexican markets.*

Clean the fish well, removing any bones and scales, and pat dry. Dust each fillet with Red Dirt Rub, then brush each with canola oil just before grilling. Grill over high heat for 3–4 minutes on each side until the fish is cooked through. The time may vary, depending on your grill.

Clean the cactus paddles well with a sharp knife, removing any small needles. Grill the cactus over high heat, just tossing it right onto the grill bars—no oil, no seasonings. Once the cactus begins to bubble slightly, turn over and season with a sprinkle of the Red Dirt Rub. As soon as both sides are lightly charred and the cactus is bubbling inside, it's ready to serve. Pull the cactus from the grill and cut into strips. Line a platter with a layer of the cactus and top with black beans; then lay the grilled striper on top. Finish with a squeeze of fresh lemon and serve.

Serves 4

Hybrid striped bass live in many of the freshwater lakes in Texas and are a fantastic fish for the grill. The flavor is extremely mild and the texture is flaky yet firm enough to hold together on the grill. Texas also has a fantastic farm-raised bass available year-round, which makes this dish easy to prepare anytime—even when the fish aren't biting. I like to serve this at outdoor parties because the fish and cactus can be easily and quickly grilled right at the last minute in front of guests, who tend to instinctively gather around a working grill.

Southwestern Grilled Tuna Salad

10 ounces fresh yellowfin
    (ahi) or blackfin tuna*
$^1/_4$ teaspoon Texas Red Dirt
    Rub Southwestern Blend
2 teaspoons extra virgin olive oil
1 small Roma tomato,
    seeded and diced
1 bunch scallions, chopped
2 ribs celery, diced
3 tablespoons mayonnaise
1 tablespoon chopped fresh cilantro
Juice of 1 lemon
$^1/_4$ teaspoon ground coriander
Pinch of cayenne pepper
Pinch of chili powder
Pinch of turmeric
$^1/_2$ teaspoon kosher salt

Lightly season the tuna with the Southwestern Blend and let it soak in for 5 minutes. Brush lightly with some of the olive oil and grill over a very hot fire for about 2 minutes per side, depending on the thickness of the tuna. Once the tuna has reached medium doneness (120 degrees internal temperature), pull from the grill and set on a plate to cool. Combine all other ingredients in a mixing bowl and stir well. Cut the cooled tuna into large cubes and mix with the dressing in the bowl. Do not break up the large pieces by overmixing.

Serves 2–3

Be sure to clean any dark bloodline away from fresh tuna steaks, as they can have overly strong flavors.

 I first came up with this dish after a deep sea fishing trip in South Padre, where the captain had managed to get us into a huge school of blackfin tuna. Driving home with a cooler filled to the brim, I wondered about making a tuna salad from these beauties. I grew up on tuna salad from a can, but this version has become my all-time favorite. Truly fresh tuna is something to be celebrated.

Crawfish and Shrimp Boil

10 pounds live crawfish

4 1/2 gallons water

2 cups kosher salt

2 pounds Texas Red Dirt Rub
   Creole Blend, divided

4 cups hot sauce

5 pounds small red or
   Yukon potatoes

4 onions, peeled and halved

3 heads of garlic, peeled and
   each head cut in half

8 pounds smoked andouille sausage,
   cut into 4–5 inch sections

10 ears fresh corn, cut
   in half lengths

10 pounds whole head-on shrimp

10 lemons

Place the live crawfish in cold water 2 hours prior to cooking, and change the water at least twice before boiling. This helps to purge the crawfish, for a cleaner flavor at the end. A clean cooler works well for storing the live "bugs," and most are equipped with a plug for easy water drainage.

Fill a very large pot (10-gallon) equipped with a strainer basket with cold water to the halfway point. Add the salt, Creole Blend (reserving 1/3 cup) and hot sauce. Add the potatoes, onions and garlic to the strainer basket and lower them into the pot; boil for 10 minutes. Pull the basket out and add to it the live crawfish, sausage, and corn, then sink it back into the liquid. Once it begins to boil again, let it cook for 10 minutes; then add in the shrimp. Boil for another 6–7 minutes, and then remove the entire basket. If the basket is not big enough to hold all of your contents, you can cook the seafood in batches. The crawfish need to cook for 16–17 minutes, but the shrimp only need 6–7 minutes of boiling. Cover an outdoor table with thick layers of newspaper, and pour the entire contents of the boil out into the center of the table in a large pile. Squeeze the lemons over the pile liberally and dust the entire pile with the reserved Creole Blend.

Serves 16–20

> *continued*

The standard "turkey fryer kit" works perfectly for this application and is the most economical way to purchase the necessary equipment for a great seafood boil. This is almost always an outdoor event, as it often gets a bit messy.

Crawfish can be purchased from many different websites when the season is in full swing and is available from some farms year-round. I like Fruge Aquafarms for my live crawfish and for great Texas shrimp as well.

Perfect Texas Brisket and Barbecue Sauce

1 whole brisket, roughly 12 pounds

6 tablespoons kosher salt

5 tablespoons granulated garlic

2 tablespoons brown sugar

3 tablespoons finely ground
  black pepper

2 tablespoons ground coriander

1/4 teaspoon ground cumin

5 tablespoons hot smoked paprika

2 tablespoons onion powder

1 tablespoon dry mustard powder

4 tablespoons chili powder

3 cups red wine vinegar

MOPPING SAUCE

2 cups apple cider vinegar

1 can or bottle Lone Star Beer

3 tablespoons Worcestershire sauce

1 cup apple juice

1/2 cup canola oil

Place the brisket on a large cutting board or sheet pan to keep the mess contained. Mix all dry ingredients together and rub the entire brisket liberally with it. Wrap the brisket in plastic and place in the fridge overnight.

Next day, let the meat sit at room temp for 2 hours before smoking. Place a water pan filled with red wine vinegar in the bottom of the smoker. Place the brisket, fat side up, in the smoker with plenty of pecan wood chips and heat up to 235 degrees. It's important to have the brisket in the oven while it's warming up, as this allows more smoke to penetrate the meat. Smoke the brisket for 12 hours at a temperature range between 225 and 235 degrees. Be sure the smoke chips stay refreshed for the entire process.

Every 2 hours, apply Mopping Sauce to the brisket. Each time you open the smoker, refresh the wood as necessary, apply the mop, and try to keep the temperature in the correct range. After 12 hours, remove the brisket and slice the meat across the grain and remove excess fat. Serve with Barbecue Sauce (see page 127).

Serves 12–15

For the mopping sauce: Whisk all ingredients together. Be sure to stir every time before using. Keep refrigerated.

BARBECUE SAUCE

6 tablespoons butter

1 large sweet onion, chopped

3 cloves garlic, minced

1/4 cup cider vinegar

3 ancho chiles, seeds and stems removed

1 teaspoon dried Mexican oregano

1/2 teaspoon dry mustard powder

1 1/2 cups ketchup

6 tablespoons brown sugar

1/3 cup bourbon

2 cups chicken stock

1/2 teaspoon kosher salt

1/2 teaspoon freshly ground black pepper

1/2 teaspoon sweet smoked paprika

1 tablespoon Worcestershire sauce

Combine all ingredients and bring to a light simmer. Simmer for 15 minutes then puree with a stick blender. Reduce until the sauce thickens slightly and serve.

Makes 4 cups

Beef brisket is the undisputed king of Texas barbecue. In the Lone Star State, if you can't make a perfect brisket, you can't barbecue—period. Brisket has to have a good dry rub and needs lots of time in a very smoky and very moist environment, for starters. An electric smoker is the easiest and most foolproof method, but a good pit is worth utilizing if you are proficient in its use. The key is to keep the temperature in the sweet spot while also applying plenty of great smoke flavor the whole time. Many competition barbecue guys (where electric smokers are banned) stay up all night long tending the fire and keeping it in that special zone.

Generally speaking, most brisket should cook for about 1 hour per pound at roughly 225 degrees. Cooking at 250 degrees is common and might work a little faster, but dropping to 200 degrees for up to 20 hours is also a favorite technique of many experienced pit men.

When checking on the brisket and applying the mop, do not be alarmed if the brisket turns black on the outside. If during the final check the brisket seems to have dried out, there is one way to resurrect the whole thing: place the whole piece into a Dutch oven and fill the bottom with 2–3 inches of red wine vinegar mixed equally with stock. Cover with a tight-fitting lid and place in a 250-degree oven for 2 hours to rehydrate the meat. This is not recommended every time but can rescue an otherwise inedible meal. The key is a moist, smoky, consistent heat for the duration of the cooking, just low and slow the whole way.

Pulled Pork with Tangy Barbecue Sauce

1 pork shoulder (Boston
   butt or pork butt),
   approximately 7 pounds
2 tablespoons kosher salt
1/2 teaspoon ground cumin
1 1/2 teaspoons ground coriander
1 teaspoon chili powder
1 tablespoon hot smoked paprika
1 tablespoon onion powder
2 teaspoons garlic powder
1/2 teaspoon dry mustard powder
1 teaspoon freshly ground
   black pepper
3 cups apple cider vinegar, divided

Clean the pork shoulder well and pat dry with paper towels. Mix all dry ingredients together and rub liberally all over the pork. Let the meat absorb the dry spices at room temperature for 3–4 hours. Prepare a smoker with pecan chips and bring the temperature up to 210 degrees. Place a water pan with 2 cups apple cider vinegar in the bottom of the smoker. Place the pork shoulder in the smoker and cook at a temperature between 200 and 210 degrees for 14 hours. The smoking chips will need to be replenished every few hours. Each time the door is opened, baste the pork with the remaining apple cider vinegar to moisten. After 14 hours, remove the pork and use two forks to pull the meat apart. Serve with Tangy Barbecue Sauce (see page 129).

Serves 12–14

Perfectly smoked pork is a thing of beauty. The pork shoulder, or Boston butt, is a large bone-in front shoulder that begins with lots of fat and connective tissue, but when cooked slow and long it melts into a tender, fall-apart texture. Pulled pork makes a great sandwich with the right barbecue sauce, or works well in tacos, burritos, and even casseroles.

The key to this kind of cooking is a temperature-controlled environment that stays right in that 200–210 range with plenty of smoke throughout the entire cooking process. Adding a water bath filled with vinegar or wine can help some smokers maintain that perfectly moist air in the sweet spot. Don't be alarmed that the outside of the pork turns pretty black by the end of the cooking. This recipe is for an approximately 7–8-pound Boston butt; any difference in size may require an adjustment in the overall time of smoking.

TANGY BARBECUE SAUCE

3 tablespoons canola oil

1 large sweet onion, chopped

1 jalapeño, seeded and diced

3 cloves garlic, minced

1/2 cup ketchup

1/2 cup canned diced tomatoes

1/3 cup apple cider vinegar

1/2 cup dry red wine

2 tablespoons turbinado sugar

2 tablespoons Worcestershire sauce

2 pasilla chiles, stems and
    seeds removed

5–6 shakes hot sauce

1 tablespoon honey

1 tablespoon plus 1 1/2
    teaspoons molasses

Juice of 2 lemons

Juice of 1 orange

1 1/2 teaspoons dry mustard powder

1 teaspoon kosher salt

1/2 teaspoon freshly ground
    black pepper

Heat the oil in a skillet over medium heat. Sauté the onion, jalapeño and garlic in oil until soft. Add remaining ingredients and bring to a light simmer. Stir well, being careful not to burn the sugars. Simmer for 12 minutes, then puree the mixture with a stick blender until smooth. Reduce until the sauce thickens slightly and serve.

Makes approximately 4 cups

Truly Texas Ribs

2 slabs spareribs or
   St. Louis–style ribs
5 tablespoons kosher salt
4 tablespoons granulated garlic
3 tablespoons brown sugar
2 tablespoons finely ground
   black pepper
2 tablespoons ground coriander
$1/2$ teaspoon ground cumin
1 tablespoon Mexican oregano
3 tablespoons hot smoked paprika
2 tablespoons onion powder
1 tablespoon dry mustard powder
6 tablespoons chili powder
3 cups apple cider vinegar
1 recipe Mopping Sauce
   (see page 125)
1 recipe Barbecue Sauce
   (see page 127)

Wash and pat dry the ribs with paper towels. Combine all dry seasonings in a mixing bowl then apply heavily to both sides of the ribs; rub the meat with as much of the dry blend as possible. Wrap the ribs in plastic wrap and leave overnight in the fridge to allow the seasonings to soak in. Bring to room temperature for 1 hour before smoking.

Prepare the smoker with pecan wood chips and place a water pan in the bottom filled with the apple cider vinegar. Place the ribs in the smoker and heat to 215 degrees. The ribs need to be in the smoker while it's heating up and should smoke for a total of 6 hours at a temperature between 215 and 225 degrees. Every 30 minutes, give the ribs a heavy application of the Mopping Sauce. With 1 hour left, baste the ribs heavily with a thick layer of Barbecue Sauce. Once finished, slice between the bones and serve with warm barbecue sauce on the side for dipping.

Serves 6–8

Ribs are sacred in Texas. Most barbecue joints are judged by their beef brisket and their pork ribs, then the other stuff all sort of falls into place. If the ribs aren't perfectly tender but still barely clinging to the bone, then the pitmaster isn't worth his salt. This recipe is perfect for large slabs of spareribs but can easily be adapted to baby back ribs as well. They will usually need to cook only about 4$1/2$ hours, but to be sure, pull at the last bone on the slab and see if it comes free easily.

Tailgating Texas Style

Tailgating in Texas has reached epic proportions.

We do not consider hot dogs on a hibachi with a side of Cheetos anything remotely worthy of the term "tailgating." When the fall season begins, the smells of mesquite, pecan or hickory wood permeate any neighborhood within three miles downwind of a football stadium before every single home game. Many hardcore tailgaters even begin the smoking process the night before a big game and set their alarms to wake up periodically through the night to keep the fire box freshly stoked with hardwood and the temperature zone in that special "sweet spot" that every barbecue veteran knows all too well.

Gameday has taken on a meaning that encompasses an entire experience that begins with the tailgating, usually several hours before kickoff. The most common tailgate food is simply anything that can be cooked on a grill, but the experts bring out their big pits for the occasion. Ribs, briskets, wings and steaks are all common, but many of today's tailgaters get more creative and choose items big on flavor, easy on last-minute prep and that can easily be picked up and eaten "caveman style" with only one hand, no utensils necessary, while holding a beverage of choice in the other, non-dominant hand.

Lamb Chop Lollipops
with Jalapeño Mustard

2 frenched* racks of lamb
   (8 bones each)
1 sprig fresh rosemary
2 tablespoons Chinese hot mustard
3 cloves garlic, minced
1 1/2 teaspoons kosher salt
1/2 teaspoon freshly ground
   black pepper
2 tablespoons olive oil

JALAPEÑO MUSTARD
1 sprig fresh rosemary
8 tablespoons Dijon mustard
1 fresh jalapeño, seeded and diced
Juice of 1 lemon

Rinse the racks of lamb lightly under cold water. Pat dry with paper towels, then cut into individual chops by cutting between the bones. Strip the rosemary leaves from the stem and chop; discard the stem. Combine the hot mustard with the garlic, salt, pepper, oil, and half of the chopped rosemary. Rub the lamb chops with this mixture and let them marinate in the fridge for 2 hours before grilling. Grill or broil the lamb chops quickly to desired doneness (I prefer medium rare, which is 125 degrees in the middle). Serve hot with Jalapeño Mustard as a dipping sauce.

For the Jalapeño Mustard: Strip the rosemary leaves from the stem and chop; discard the stem. Combine the rosemary with the Dijon mustard, jalapeño, and lemon juice.

Serves 6–8

Meat cut away to expose part of the bone.

 If I had to choose just one thing to serve at a tailgate this would be it. I love the idea of meaty little lamb chops eaten caveman style and biting right into them. And the acidic Dijon mustard, just strong enough to tickle the nose a bit, with generous amounts of rosemary and jalapeño, really pairs perfectly with these little chops.

Shrimp and Cactus Tacos

2 cactus paddles*
Vegetable oil spray
Pinch of kosher salt
Pinch of freshly ground pepper
1 pound baby gulf shrimp
1 cup Guajillo Chile Sauce
10 white corn tortillas
10 ounces Monterey Jack cheese
12–14 sprigs fresh cilantro

Clean the cactus paddles very well of all needles with a sharp knife. Spray lightly with oil and grill over a hot fire with a pinch of salt and pepper on each side. Cook until each side lightly blisters and browns and the inside begins to bubble. Remove from the grill and cut into large dice. Simmer the baby shrimp in Guajillo Chile Sauce for 1–2 minutes, until the shrimp are just cooked. Place the tortillas on a hot flat surface with just a light spray of oil, flip after 30 seconds, and top each with shredded cheese. As soon as the cheese begins to melt, add a spoonful of shrimp in chili sauce, a sprig of fresh cilantro, and a few squares of cactus. Fold over into a soft taco and serve.

Serves 4–6

GUAJILLO CHILE SAUCE

$^1/_2$ pound dried guajillo chiles, seeds and stems removed
6 Roma tomatoes
$^1/_2$ poblano pepper, stem and seeds removed
1 red bell pepper
1 jalapeño, seeds and veins removed
10 sprigs fresh cilantro
1 small white onion
3 cloves garlic
1 tablespoon kosher salt

Place the guajillo chiles in a medium-size saucepot and add in just enough water to cover. Bring to a simmer, cover, and let simmer on low for 2 hours. Add the remaining ingredients and continue to simmer uncovered for 30–45 minutes more. Puree well with a stick blender and strain. Adjust the thickness of the sauce by adding water if it's too thick, or reducing further if it's too thin.

Makes 3 cups

Called nopales in Mexican markets.

The Guajillo Chile Sauce that I use in this dish is one of the most versatile sauces that I make. It works for enchiladas, chicken, and any number of other dishes. The tricky thing about guajillos is their stubborn fibrous nature. They take about 2 hours to finally give in and rehydrate, but the resulting flavor is robust and earthy and one of my absolute favorites.

Grilled Shrimp with Chimichurri Sauce

6 large rosemary sprigs
1 pound wild-caught gulf shrimp (10–
   15 count), peeled and deveined
1 teaspoon Texas Red Dirt Rub
   Southwestern Blend
Olive oil spray
1 cup Chimichurri Sauce

Remove most of the rosemary leaves from their stems. Soak the stems in cold water to keep them from drying out and burning on the grill. Skewer the shrimp onto the rosemary stems, leaving plenty of space in between for even cooking. Season the shrimp well with the Red Dirt Rub on all sides, then lightly spray with olive oil and grill. They should cook for about 1½–2 minutes per side. Remove and top with Chimichurri Sauce, or serve it alongside as a dipping sauce.

Serves 6

CHIMICHURRI SAUCE

1 bunch fresh Italian parsley,
   chopped (stems removed)
1 large shallot, minced
3 cloves garlic, minced
Juice of 3 lemons
4 tablespoons red wine vinegar
1 tablespoon kosher salt
½ teaspoon hot smoked paprika
½ teaspoon mustard powder
1 cup extra virgin olive oil

Combine all ingredients in a mixing bowl and whisk together well. Let stand at room temperature for at least 1 hour before serving.

Makes 2 cups

 I first fell in love with chimichurri on a hunting trip with my brother and dad in Argentina. It seemed that every meal in the whole country had a bowl of chimichurri as a condiment. We joked that this was like the Argentinian version of salsa. As soon as I got home, I began experimenting with flavors to make a chimichurri that I felt went well with almost anything that comes off of a grill.

Jalapeño Pickled Shrimp

1 large sweet onion, sliced (I prefer
   the Texas 1015 when in season)

2 fresh jalapeños, sliced

1 1/2 cups white vinegar

4 tablespoons olive oil

2 tablespoons Worcestershire sauce

2 tablespoons dry mustard powder

2 tablespoons garlic powder

1 tablespoon onion powder

1 tablespoon dried dill

1 tablespoon dried chives

1 tablespoon kosher salt

10–15 whole black peppercorns

5 bay leaves

1 1/2 pounds cooked gulf shrimp,
   peeled and deveined,
   tails left on

Combine all ingredients except the shrimp and refrigerate overnight. Pour over shrimp and allow them to pickle for at least 45 minutes before serving.

Serves 8–10

 My dad first made this recipe back in the late 1970s, and it's still a crowd favorite around town. His version uses Good Seasons cheese garlic packets as a shortcut and also includes a jar of pickled cocktail onions. I love his original dish, but I have also tweaked it over the years to my personal taste. Either way, this dish is packed with intense flavors!

Smoked Chicken Salad with Pecans

1 whole Pecan-Smoked Spicy
   Chicken (see page 78)

$^1/_4$ cup chopped pecans

3 ribs celery, diced

4 scallions (green parts
   only), chopped

1 tablespoon extra virgin olive oil

1 tablespoon plus 1 $^1/_2$ teaspoons
   Texas honey

$^1/_4$ cup mayonnaise

1 teaspoon Texas Red Dirt
   Rub Creole Blend

Let the smoked chicken cool enough to handle, then pick all the meat from the bird. Remove any skin; tear all white and dark meat by hand into rough pieces and place in a mixing bowl. Add all other ingredients and mix with your hands to incorporate. Do not smash up the chicken or overmix; just leave the pieces in large rough form.

Makes 4 cups

 This is the most flavorful chicken salad that I know of, emphasizing the fresh flavor of great chicken. I use free-range birds from Dominion Farms, which have superior flavor and always deliver juicy perfection when smoked or roasted. This salad is perfect as a topper for fresh baby spinach or greens, is delicious served over vine-ripened tomato slices, and also makes a fantastic sandwich. For tailgating crowds, I like to put the salad on little slider rolls. It's big on flavor but not too filling.

Texas Beer Can Chicken

1 full-flavored beer (I prefer
    Rahr Ugly Pug)
3 tablespoons Texas Red Dirt Rub
    Southwestern Blend, divided
1 tablespoon Worcestershire sauce
$1/3$ cup apple juice
Juice of 2 limes
1 whole chicken,
    approximately 5 pounds

Open the beer and pour half of the contents into a chilled glass (enjoy!). Combine the remaining beer with 1 tablespoon of the Southwestern Blend and all other ingredients (except the chicken, of course) and mix. Pour the mix into the center of a beer can roaster. If using a beer can instead of a roaster, puncture the top of an empty can with a church key opener 3 or 4 times, then pour in the mixture. Wash and dry the whole chicken and remove anything that might be inside. Be sure to remove as much extra fat as possible. Season the chicken inside and out with the remaining Southwestern Blend. Rub the seasonings under the skin for a better infusion.

Place the seasoned chicken upright over the can or roaster so that the can stands up inside the body cavity. The contents inside the can will constantly baste the bird and flavor it from the inside out. Grill with the lid down over medium heat for approximately 1–1$1/2$ hours. Remove from the heat carefully and carve while the bird is still standing up to avoid spilling the hot beer marinade. (To achieve a natural smoke flavor using a gas grill, place the bird over one side turned to low and add a few wood chips wrapped in foil over the other side turned to high. It's usually very helpful to place a drip pan under the cooking bird to keep the drippings from either flaring up or putting out the fire. Do not cook over high direct heat, or the chicken will cook very unevenly.)

Serves 2–4

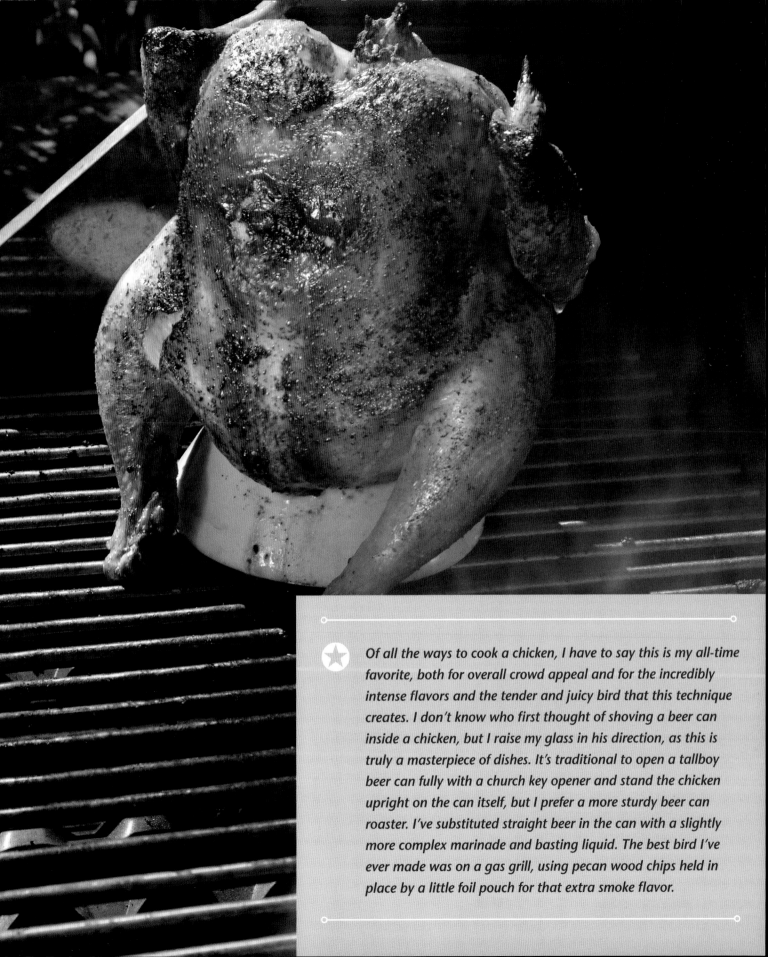

Of all the ways to cook a chicken, I have to say this is my all-time favorite, both for overall crowd appeal and for the incredibly intense flavors and the tender and juicy bird that this technique creates. I don't know who first thought of shoving a beer can inside a chicken, but I raise my glass in his direction, as this is truly a masterpiece of dishes. It's traditional to open a tallboy beer can fully with a church key opener and stand the chicken upright on the can itself, but I prefer a more sturdy beer can roaster. I've substituted straight beer in the can with a slightly more complex marinade and basting liquid. The best bird I've ever made was on a gas grill, using pecan wood chips held in place by a little foil pouch for that extra smoke flavor.

Frito Pie

2 pounds beef sirloin

3 teaspoons Texas Red Dirt
    Rub Creole Blend

1 red bell pepper, diced

1 poblano pepper, diced

2 cloves garlic, minced

1 small sweet onion, diced

2 ribs celery, diced

2 teaspoons canola oil

1 1/2 cups Guajillo Chile
    Sauce (see page 137)

1 jalapeño, diced (seeds optional)

2 teaspoons chili powder

1/4 teaspoon ground cumin

Pinch of ground cloves

2 teaspoons canola oil

12 small bags Frito corn chips

RECOMMENDED GARNISHES

Sour cream

Diced jalapeños

Fresh cilantro

Shredded cheddar cheese

Diced tomatoes

Chopped onion or scallions

Season the sirloin with 2 teaspoons of the Creole Blend and either place in a smoker or on a grill over hardwood. Cook until medium done, then remove and let cool. Once cooled, cut into small dice, reserving any juices that may run out.

In a large pan, sauté the bell and poblano peppers, garlic, onion, and celery in oil until they have all softened. Season with the remaining teaspoon of Creole Blend, then add in the diced sirloin and any juices. Add in the Guajillo Chile Sauce and all remaining ingredients except corn chips, and bring to a simmer. Simmer until the entire mixture begins to thicken slightly. Tear the ends off the Frito bags and pour one large spoonful of the chili mixture into each bag over the corn chips; garnish as desired.

Serves 12

 The Frito Pie Bar is one of my favorite buffet items to set up when tailgating. Each person can grab a bag of Fritos, fill it with chili, then garnish however they like and eat right out of the bag with a spoon—no plates needed, no mess to clean up. The beef can even be cooked ahead of time, leaving very little work to be done as game time approaches.

Grilled Watermelon with Tequila Lime Vinaigrette

6–8 red watermelon slices,
    1 1/2 inches thick
6–8 yellow watermelon slices,
    1 1/2 inches thick
Pinch kosher salt

Place the watermelon slices on a very hot grill and cook for 15–20 seconds, then turn 45 degrees and place back down (without turning over). This will make the crisscross grill mark pattern. After another 15–20 seconds, turn the watermelon over and repeat. Give each slice a very light pinch of kosher salt after turning over. Do not try to cook the watermelon, just get nice dark grill marks on the outside and stop. The melon should still have great crunch in the middle. Arrange the slices on a platter, then pour plenty of Tequila Lime Vinaigrette over them.

TEQUILA LIME VINAIGRETTE
5–6 sprigs fresh cilantro
2–3 sprigs fresh mint
Juice of 2 1/2 limes
3 tablespoons white tequila
1 jalapeño, seeded and diced
2 cloves garlic, minced
1 teaspoon dry mustard powder
2 tablespoons agave nectar or honey
6 ounces canola oil
1/2 teaspoon kosher salt
Pinch freshly ground black pepper

Tear the cilantro and mint by hand into rough leaves, then place in a mixing bowl. Add all remaining ingredients and whisk together well. Let sit for 15–20 minutes before serving.

Makes 6–8

The taste of grilled watermelon is hard to describe. As the melon grills, some of the sugars caramelize and the slices become sweeter and more complex in flavor. It may seem odd to put watermelon on the grill, but try it once and taste what you've been missing. The vinaigrette with a hint of tequila puts this particular dish right over the top! It makes a vibrant platter of color that looks great at a tailgate party, where huge platters of meat usually dominate. It's also a great finger food that invites everyone to just pick up and enjoy without utensils or plates.

Barbecued Shrimp Quesadillas

1 pound gulf shrimp (26–30
  count), peeled and deveined
1 recipe Sweet and Tangy
  Barbecue Sauce
2 1/2 teaspoons butter, divided
5 large flour tortillas
1/2 cup grated Monterey Jack cheese

Add the shrimp to the barbecue sauce and
bring to a light simmer. Cook just until the
shrimp are done, about 2–3 minutes, then
set aside and keep warm. Using 1/2 teaspoon
of butter per tortilla, add a little butter to
a preheated flat-top surface, then top with
a flour tortilla and sprinkle on some of the
cheese. As soon as the cheese begins to melt,
top with a heaping spoonful of barbecued
shrimp with sauce and fold the tortilla in
half. Continue to cook until the tortillas
have nicely browned on each side, then
remove and cut each quesadilla into three
triangles to serve.

Serves 4–6

SWEET AND TANGY BARBECUE SAUCE
2 shallots, minced
3 cloves garlic, minced
3 tablespoons canola oil
1 (14-ounce) can diced tomatoes with juice
2 tablespoons soy sauce
1/2 teaspoon ancho chili powder
2 teaspoons Mexican oregano
1 1/2 teaspoons ground black pepper
2 tablespoons honey
2 tablespoons plus 1 1/2 teaspoons
  cider vinegar
1 teaspoon red chili paste
  (also called sambal)
1 tablespoon plus 1 1/2 teaspoons
  brown sugar

Sauté the shallots and garlic in oil until soft. Add all
remaining ingredients and simmer covered for 15–20
minutes, until the sauce begins to thicken. Puree with a
stick blender until smooth, then strain.

Makes 3 cups

*This is an easy and popular dish at my tailgates, since most of the work can be
done well ahead of time. I throw a flat cast-iron griddle down over half of the
grill to make the most consistent quesadillas. The sauce can be completely done
ahead of time, leaving only the shrimp to be simmered in the sauce while the
cheese heats and melts over the warm tortillas.*

Tenderloin Sliders

1 whole beef tenderloin
(approximately 4–5 pounds)
Texas Red Dirt Rub Creole
Blend, to taste
Nonstick grilling spray
36 mini rolls
3 boxes Boursin cheese with
Garlic and Fine Herbs
4 red bell peppers, roasted,
peeled, and cut into strips
2 bunches fresh arugula

Clean the tenderloin and cut into small medallions, 2–3 ounces each. Season lightly on each side with the Creole Blend and lightly spray with nonstick grilling spray. With the grill on its highest setting, grill the medallions very quickly. This should only take about 1 minute per side on a hot grill. Cut the rolls in half and spread cheese on both halves of each roll. Place a hot medallion of tenderloin in each sandwich and top with roasted red pepper strips and a few leaves of arugula.

Makes 30–35 sliders

When the tenderloin is cut into small medallions like this, the cooking time is very short and easy, leaving the cook more time to enjoy the party. And these little sliders are jam-packed with robust flavors—real crowd pleasers.

Wild Game, Huntin' Season

Wild game has always played a major role in my culinary life, starting back in my earliest years.

Even before I was old enough to hold or fire a gun, I walked with my dad and older brother through the woods and fields, practicing gun safety with my toy model while watching the bird dogs work the field edges in the cool fall early mornings of north Texas. At the end of the hunt, hopefully a limit of birds in hand, I reveled in the fact that even though I was too young to shoot, I could still help clean the birds. And a successful Saturday morning hunt almost assured a fried quail and grits breakfast on Sunday morning.

That's how much of my childhood and formative years were spent, trouncing through fields and waters, harvesting birds and beasts for the table. As we hunted more, we worked harder on new preparations. Making a dinner of the game I harvested and cooked myself, then served to neighbors and friends who actually enjoyed it and went back for seconds was about as fulfilling and prideful as anything in the world to this teenager.

For all of those hunters out there, or their frustrated wives who wonder why everyone else seems to like the taste of their wild game rather than just suffer through it, this chapter is for you. These are some of my favorite ways to tame the wild.

Pheasant Strips with Jalapeño and Bacon Cream Gravy

3 pheasants, breast meat only

$^1/_2$ cup buttermilk

1 tablespoon hot sauce

1 cup flour

1 tablespoon Texas Red Dirt
  Rub Creole Blend

1 recipe Jalapeño and Bacon
  Cream Gravy (see page 106)

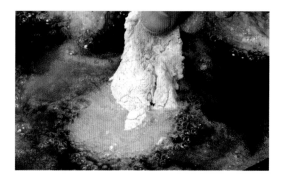

Cut each pheasant breast half into 3 or 4 long strips by cutting directly across the grain of the meat. Combine the strips with the buttermilk and hot sauce in a ziplock bag and refrigerate overnight. Be sure the contents are well mixed, and from time to time, pick up the bag and shake to ensure the strips are evenly coated.

Combine the flour and Creole Blend together. Pull out the strips one at a time, allowing the excess buttermilk to drip off, and dredge them in the flour mixture; make sure each pheasant strip is completely coated in the seasoned flour. Fry in 350-degree oil until brown and crisp on both sides. This should take roughly 2–3 minutes, depending on the size and thickness of the pheasant. Drain the strips on paper towels and serve with Jalapeño and Bacon Cream Gravy for dipping.

Serves 6–8

 Pheasant is a white-meat bird that's easy for everyone to like but also easy to overcook and dry out, so special care must be taken to avoid this. The dish can either be deep-fried or pan-fried. This method of frying the strips quickly, just until the coating is lightly golden brown, assures that the meat inside will be done precisely when the coating is finished. It's important to cut the strips into pretty uniform sizes and to maintain the oil at 350 degrees. If the oil gets too hot, the coating will brown too quickly without cooking the pheasant, but if too cold, the strips will overcook and soak through with grease.

Smoked Pheasant Dip

2 whole pheasants
2 teaspoons kosher salt
$^{1}/_{4}$ teaspoon cayenne pepper
3 large pitted green olives
2 tablespoons chopped shallot
8 ounces soft cream cheese
$^{3}/_{4}$ cup heavy cream
Juice of 1 lemon
1 tablespoon chopped fresh thyme
1 tablespoon chopped
  fresh tarragon
1 tablespoon chopped fresh basil

Rinse the whole pheasants well under cold water and pick clean of any shot or extra feathers. Pat dry with paper towels, then season lightly with salt and pepper and place in a smoker at 250 degrees. Cook for 1$^{1}/_{2}$–2 hours, until cooked through. Remove and pick all of the meat from the carcasses as soon as the birds are cool enough to handle. Place all of the meat, olives, and shallots in a food processor; pulse several times to begin breaking up the meat. Add all remaining ingredients and puree until a smooth texture is achieved. Serve with assorted crackers and flatbreads for dipping.

Makes 6 cups

 This simple variation of pâté is an elegant and classy way to spruce up pheasants from a hunting trip. The meat of pheasant has tremendous flavor but can often become a bit dry when cooked. This recipe takes care of the dryness by adding in many moist components while still spotlighting the flavor of wild pheasant.

Venison Quesadillas

1 pound venison backstrap
  or back leg meat

MARINADE
1 ounce red wine
1 ounce red wine vinegar
1 tablespoon soy sauce
2–3 shakes hot sauce
2 cloves garlic, minced
$1/4$ teaspoon brown sugar
2 teaspoons olive oil

$2^1/_2$ teaspoons butter
5 large flour tortillas
$1/2$ cup grated cheddar cheese
1 jalapeño, finely diced

GARNISHES
Sour cream
Guacamole
Salsa
Chopped fresh jalapeño

Clean the venison well and be sure that any connective tissue or silver skin is removed. Cut the venison down to $1/2$-inch thickness for grilling. Any size pieces will work, as long as they are not too thick. Combine the venison with all other ingredients and let marinate for at least 2 hours in a ziplock bag. Remove the venison pieces from the bag and shake off any excess marinade. Grill over a very hot fire for roughly 1 minute per side, just until it is well seared on the outside but still medium-rare in the middle. Pull the meat from the grill and let rest for 8–10 minutes before cutting into medium-size dice.

Using $1/2$ teaspoon of butter per tortilla, add a little butter to a preheated flat-top surface, then top with a flour tortilla and sprinkle on some of the cheese. As soon as the cheese begins to melt, add several of the venison pieces and a little jalapeño, then fold the tortilla in half. Continue to cook until the tortillas have browned nicely on both sides, then remove and cut into triangles. Garnish and serve.

Serves 4–6

For anyone that might not be ready to try venison all by itself, this is a great introductory dish. With an intensely flavored marinade, grilled venison makes a perfect rich component to great quesadillas. Be careful not to overcook the venison, and let it rest before slicing to bring out the best flavor possible.

This dish always reminds me of spring, when the Tom turkeys are strutting their stuff and gobbling incessantly. This recipe is a kid pleaser, with a perfectly crispy outer texture and succulent, tender white meat inside. It's very important to cut the turkey breast directly across the grain of the meat, against the long muscle fibers. If the strips are cut with the grain, the texture can become very stringy and tough.

The breast meat from wild turkeys works exceptionally well for this recipe, but the legs will need a different type of preparation, such as braising or stewing, since they are somewhat tougher and more spindly.

Wild Turkey Tenders

2 pounds wild turkey breast meat

1 cup buttermilk

3 tablespoons hot sauce

2 cups flour

2 tablespoons Texas Red Dirt
   Rub Creole Blend, divided

3 eggs

1/4 cup plus 2 tablespoons milk

2 cups panko bread crumbs

Oil for deep-frying

Cut the turkey breasts into thin strips by cutting directly across the grain of the meat. Combine the strips with the buttermilk and hot sauce in a ziplock bag and refrigerate overnight. Be sure the contents are well mixed, and from time to time, pick up the bag and shake to ensure the strips are evenly coated.

Combine the flour and 1 tablespoon of the Creole Blend in a shallow rectangular pan. Crack the eggs and combine them with the milk; pour into a second rectangular pan. Combine the panko bread crumbs with the other tablespoon of seasonings and place them in a third pan.

Remove the tenders from the buttermilk mixture and drain off any excess buttermilk. Dip them into the flour mixture and coat well, then dip into the egg mixture and coat well, then coat in the bread crumbs. (This is known as the standard breading procedure; flour, egg, bread crumbs.) Deep-fry in 350-degree oil until brown and crisp on all sides. This should take roughly 2–3 minutes, depending on the size and thickness of the turkey strips. Drain the strips on paper towels and serve with Southwestern Buttermilk Dressing (see page 117).

Serves 6–8

Dove season is the first hunting season to open each year. Many father/son or father/daughter trips are planned for this opening weekend with good friends camping out to celebrate this special time. I love this recipe cooked right over a campfire in the great outdoors. The marinade can be made ahead of time and brought to the campsite in a plastic bottle or ziplock bag. The gravy can also be made ahead and reheated as needed. The rest just requires a little luck and a few good shots.

Dove Kebobs with Mushroom Gravy

15 doves
2 tablespoons plus
   1 1/2 teaspoons olive oil
2 cloves garlic, minced
2 teaspoons soy sauce
1/2 teaspoon cracked black pepper
1 tablespoon red wine vinegar
2 teaspoons honey
4 strips bacon

Clean the doves well and cut the breast portions off each side of the breast bone with a sharp paring knife. Place the meat in a mixing bowl. In another bowl, combine oil, garlic, soy sauce, pepper, vinegar, and honey. Mix well and pour over the dove pieces; coat well. Let marinate in the fridge for at least 2 hours.

Soak 6–8 bamboo skewers in water for 15–20 minutes. Meanwhile, cut the bacon into small squares roughly the same length as the dove breast pieces. Skewer the breasts and bacon, alternating between the two. Be sure to skewer them loosely, leaving a little room between the pieces to facilitate even cooking. Grill the skewers over a very hot fire for 1–2 minutes per side, until medium rare. Overcooking will result in dry and strongly flavored meat. Slide the meat off of the skewers and serve with Mushroom Gravy.

Serves 6

MUSHROOM GRAVY

2 strips bacon, diced
1/2 cup finely diced mushrooms
2 tablespoons minced shallot
1 tablespoon flour
1 tablespoon butter
1 1/4 cups half-and-half
3–4 fresh sage leaves, chopped
1/2 teaspoon kosher salt
1/4 teaspoon cracked black pepper

Begin by rendering the bacon in a large pan. When the bacon has mostly rendered but is not yet crispy, add the mushrooms and shallots. Sauté for 2 minutes, then sprinkle in the flour; add the butter and whisk. Cook until the flour just lightly begins to brown, then add in the half-and-half. Whisk quickly to combine and continue whisking until the gravy reaches a simmer. Add the sage, salt, and pepper, and simmer until the gravy reaches the perfect thickness for dipping. If it comes out too thin, keep reducing until it thickens. If too thick, add a touch more half-and-half to thin it out.

Makes 2 cups

Venison Meatball Sliders

1 pound venison meat

1/2 pound pork shoulder

2 eggs

1 shallot, minced

4 cloves garlic, minced

6 tablespoons grated Parmesan cheese

1/3 cup panko bread crumbs

1 tablespoon plus 1 1/2 teaspoons
   Dijon mustard

1 tablespoon chopped fresh parsley

1 tablespoon chopped fresh basil

1 1/2 teaspoons chopped fresh oregano

1/2 teaspoon ground black pepper

1 teaspoon kosher salt

14–16 mini buns or rolls

Grated mozzarella cheese for garnish

Clean the venison very well, removing all fat and silver skin, then cut into large chunks. Cut the pork shoulder into large chunks as well. Toss all ingredients together (except for the rolls and cheese garnish) in a large mixing bowl and combine well. Grind all ingredients together through the smallest plate on your grinder. Mix well, then test one meatball for seasonings by quickly sautéing a small portion in a pan and tasting it; adjust the seasonings if necessary. Form the mixture into golf ball–size meatballs by rolling between your hands. Deep-fry the meatballs for 1 minute in 350-degree oil; then remove and let the meatballs drain.

Place the meatballs gently in the simmering Marinara Sauce; simmer for 15–20 minutes, until cooked through. Serve on mini buns or small rolls with an extra spoonful of Marinara Sauce for each one. Add a touch of grated mozzarella cheese to the top of each meatball, if desired.

Makes 14–16 sliders

MARINARA SAUCE

1 yellow onion, chopped

3 cloves garlic, minced

2 ribs celery, chopped

3 tablespoons olive oil

1/2 cup dry red wine

4 cups canned diced tomatoes with juice

2 teaspoons chopped fresh oregano

1 teaspoon chopped fresh basil

1/2 teaspoon chopped fresh thyme

1 teaspoon kosher salt

Pinch of freshly ground black pepper

In a large saucepot, sauté the onion, garlic, and celery in olive oil until soft. Deglaze with red wine and reduce until the pan is almost dry. Add the tomatoes, bring to a simmer for 8 minutes, and then puree with a stick blender until smooth. Stir in the herbs and seasonings; simmer for an additional 3–5 minutes, then serve.

Makes 5 cups

This is an easy way to get everyone in your family to enjoy venison, especially those that might be a little squeamish. The meatballs, when cooked in this rich sauce, can easily be served atop spaghetti with some grated Parmesan, but my preference is these little one-handed sliders. It's also a great dish for tailgates or around the campfire.

Venison Chili

3 pounds venison meat

1 1/2 pounds pork shoulder

3 tablespoons canola oil

2 tablespoons Texas Red Dirt
　　Rub Southwestern Blend

3 tablespoons plus 1 1/2 teaspoons
　　chili powder

1 tablespoon smoked hot paprika

1 teaspoon ground cumin

1 teaspoon ground coriander

Pinch of ground cloves

2 teaspoons kosher salt

1 teaspoon cracked black pepper

1 teaspoon Worcestershire sauce

5–6 dashes hot sauce

3 large sweet onions, diced medium

7 cloves garlic, minced

2 jalapeños, seeded and diced

5 tablespoons crushed tortilla chips (a
　　rolling pin works well for crushing
　　them, or just crush by hand)

1 (6-ounce) can tomato paste

3 bottles Shiner Bock Beer

Clean the venison well, removing any fat or connective tissue. Cut the venison and pork shoulder into large chunks and grind together, using the large-holed plate on your grinder. Brown the meat in hot oil in a large Dutch oven–style pot. Once the meat is well browned, add all of the spices and flavorings, then the onion, garlic, jalapeño, and tortilla chips. Sauté together for 3–4 minutes. Add the tomato paste and the beer. Bring to a light simmer, cover tightly with a lid, and simmer on low for 2 hours. Remove the lid and stir to check the consistency. Once the chili has reached a thick texture, it's ready to serve. If it seems too thin, simmer without the lid until it thickens up.

Serves 10–12

 Venison is one of the first meats I ever learned to cook by myself, because the pride of harvesting your own deer is something I needed to share with others. By itself, venison can be somewhat strongly flavored, but with a little coaxing and the right blend of seasonings, it's luxurious. I tend to use cuts from the front legs or back legs for chili, saving the loins for grilling or sautéing. It's very important to trim the venison well of any fat or connective tissue. The pork shoulder, on the other hand, should be cut as is, leaving all of the fat and connective tissue in the dish.

Venison Burgers

2 pounds venison meat

1/2 pound pork shoulder

1/2 pound slab bacon

1 tablespoon Worcestershire sauce

1/2 teaspoon onion powder

Pinch of cayenne pepper

1/2 teaspoon garlic powder

2 tablespoons Dijon mustard

2 teaspoons hot sauce

1 teaspoon kosher salt

1/2 teaspoon freshly ground
   black pepper

OPTIONAL TOPPINGS

Bacon

Cheddar cheese

Guacamole

Clean the venison well and remove any fat or connective tissue. Cut the venison, pork shoulder, and bacon into large chunks. Combine all ingredients together in a large mixing bowl and let marinate for 1 hour in the refrigerator. Grind everything together using the small plate on your grinder. Form into burger patties by hand, and grill or pan-sear. Cook to medium (135 degrees internal temperature) then remove from the grill and top with your favorite cheese or burger toppings. My favorite is bacon, cheddar, guacamole burgers!

Serves 8

 Venison is an incredibly rich meat but also quite lean. It's extremely important to take proper care of your venison in the field, as well as to trim away all fat and connective tissues when processing. Adding pork and pork fat helps give a somewhat dry meat more juice and gives a more approachable texture to these burgers. Anyone who says they don't like venison has probably never had it dressed up quite like this before.

Quail and Shiitake Spring Rolls

8 ounces quail meat, cut
    off the bone
1 poblano pepper, stems
    and seeds removed
6–8 shiitake mushroom caps
2 teaspoons olive oil
2 cloves garlic, minced
1 shallot, finely diced
1/2 teaspoon kosher salt
Pinch of freshly ground
    black pepper
1 teaspoon chopped fresh ginger
4–5 sprigs fresh cilantro, chopped
Juice of 1 lime
1 package spring roll dough
    (found in the freezer section)
1 egg yolk, whisked
Oil for deep-frying

Cut the quail, poblano and mushroom caps into julienne strips. In a large sauté pan, brown the quail meat in oil quickly, then add the poblano, mushrooms, garlic, and shallot. Sauté all together until the mushrooms begin to soften; season with salt, pepper, and ginger. Stir in the cilantro and lime juice and remove from the heat. Let cool in the refrigerator.

Once the mixture has cooled, place 2 squares of defrosted spring roll dough on a flat surface. Place 2 heaping spoonfuls of the quail mixture in the middle, fold in the sides, then roll and use a touch of egg yolk to seal the edges. Let the rolls rest in the fridge for at least 10 minutes, then deep-fry in 350-degree vegetable oil until lightly brown and crisp on all sides, approximately 2–3 minutes (turn when the bottom browns; they tend to float and cook unevenly if left alone). Drain on paper towels, cut on a diagonal with a serrated knife, and serve with Sweet and Hot Chili Sauce (see page 172).

Serves 6

> *continued*

I'm not usually one for Asian-inspired dishes, but for spring rolls I'll stretch a little. I love the way spring roll dough forms a light and crispy texture when fried, and when dipped into this spicy yet sweet sauce, it really works for me.

SWEET AND HOT CHILI SAUCE

1 shallot, finely diced

2 cloves garlic, minced

1 jalapeño, seeds removed, diced

$1/2$ teaspoon olive oil

1 tablespoon red chili
    paste (sambal)

2 tablespoons soy sauce

$3/4$ cup chicken stock

$1/2$ cup apricot jam

1 teaspoon chopped fresh ginger

Sauté the shallot, garlic, and jalapeño in oil until lightly softened. Add the remaining ingredients and simmer lightly for 10 minutes, until the sauce has slightly thickened.

Makes 1 $1/2$ cups

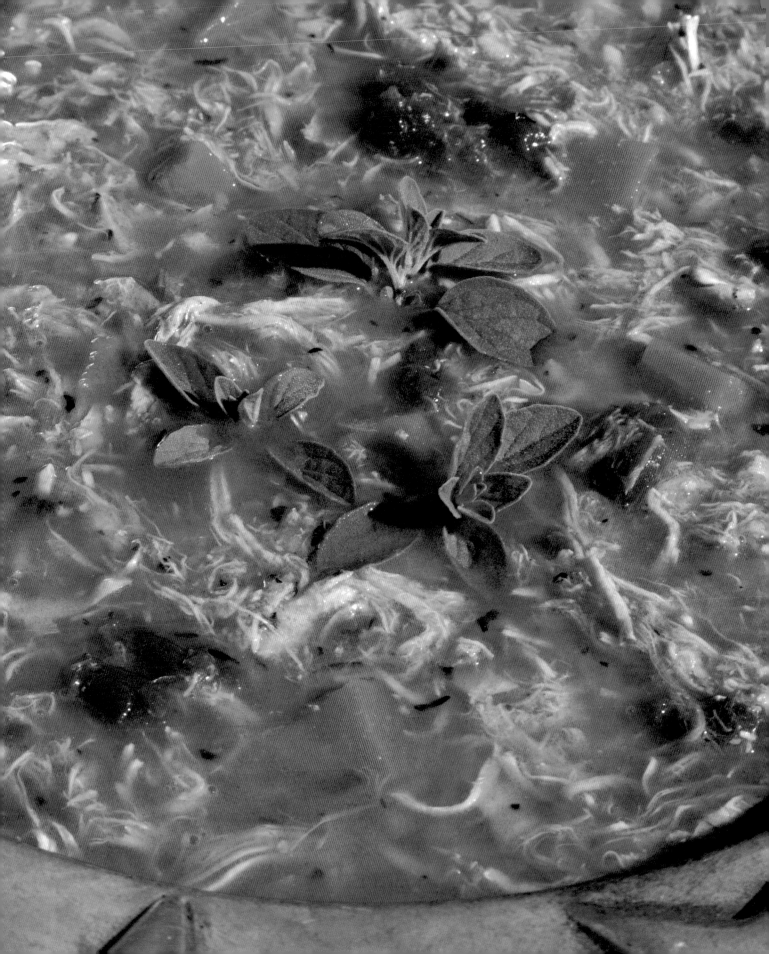

Hearty Game Bird Stew

3 pounds white-meat game birds
   (quail, chukar, pheasant)
1 tablespoon plus 1 1/2 teaspoons
   kosher salt
1/2 teaspoon freshly ground
   black pepper
2 tablespoons olive oil
1/3 cup dry white wine
3 quarts chicken stock, divided
1 large yellow onion, diced
2 ribs celery, diced
1 large carrot, peeled
   and diced large
4 cloves garlic, minced
1 (16-ounce) can diced
   tomatoes with juice
1 1/2 teaspoons dried thyme
1 1/2 teaspoons dried basil
1 1/2 teaspoons dried oregano
1/3 cup long-grain white rice
Fresh herbs for garnish

Season all of the birds lightly with salt and pepper, then heat the oil in a large Dutch oven and brown the meat on all sides. Add the wine and 1 cup of chicken stock; bring to a simmer. Cover tightly and cook on low for 1 1/2 hours. Remove the birds from the pot and let cool slightly, then pick all the meat from the bones and tear into bite-size rough pieces. Return the meat to the pot and add in all remaining ingredients. Simmer uncovered on low for 45 minutes to 1 hour, until the all ingredients are cooked through. Garnish with your favorite fresh herbs.

Serves 10–12

Many hunters in Texas enjoy hunting preserves, where a mixed bag of birds is likely to be harvested. This recipe is great with any white-meat game birds and can serve a large group of guests. The labor involved in picking through the meat will take some time, but it makes for a more refined and user-friendly final dish.

Southwestern Sides

What goes under or alongside the meat can be just as important as the meat itself on a Texas plate. Of all the dishes that I've ever served up at my restaurant (over 350 to date), the single most requested recipe has been my grits.

I serve three different flavors of grits right now, so I included a couple of my favorites in this chapter. The same old meat-and-potatoes approach is not really good enough anymore to satisfy today's Texas appetite. Both meat and potatoes need some added kick and special attention to get any recognition in today's world.

While meats, poultry, and fish generally receive the spotlight at most meals, the sides should never be overlooked when planning a perfect meal. To show off your culinary talents, never be afraid to spruce up your sides. I like to think of potatoes, grits, and rice as almost a blank canvas, something that can be turned into just about anything, with a little creative thought. The sides in this chapter can be used to enhance other main dishes, or some can even stand alone as great snacks or lighter dishes all by themselves.

Texas Confetti Rice

2 ears fresh corn, husked

2 shallots, finely diced

2 cloves garlic, finely diced

2 teaspoons butter

2 cups Texmati white rice

3 1/2 cups vegetable stock or water

1 1/2 teaspoons kosher salt

1 red bell pepper, finely diced

1 medium-size carrot, finely diced

2 ribs celery, finely diced

Grill the corn ears until the kernels are a nice golden brown on all sides, then cut corn from the cob. In a sauce pot, sauté the shallots and garlic in butter for 2–3 minutes, then add the rice and stir to coat in the butter. Pour in the stock and bring to a light simmer. Add the salt. Cook on low for 15 minutes partially covered (place the lid on, but leave a little opening). Do not stir while rice is cooking. At the end, add in the remaining vegetables and stir one time then serve.

Makes 6 cups

 It's important not to disturb rice when it's cooking. Stirring too much will cause it to become a sticky mess. Once the rice is cooked, add in the finely diced veggies and stir just once. This dish makes a great side for pork and seafood dishes, adding more complex flavors and textures to simple rice.

Marinated Tomato and Sweet Onion Salad

1 tablespoon white wine vinegar

1 tablespoon lemon juice

1 teaspoon Dijon mustard

4–5 shakes hot sauce

5 tablespoons extra virgin olive oil

1 clove garlic

$1/2$ teaspoon dried oregano

1 teaspoon kosher salt

$1/2$ teaspoon cracked black pepper

$1/4$ teaspoon celery seed

$1/2$ teaspoon dried thyme

4 large ripe tomatoes,
   cut into wedges

1 small to medium sweet
   onion, julienned

6–7 large fresh basil leaves

Combine all vinaigrette ingredients (everything except the tomatoes, onions, and basil) in a blender and puree until smooth. Let sit for 1 hour, then dress the tomatoes and onions and marinate for 1 additional hour at room temperature. Add freshly torn basil leaves just before serving.

Serves 6–8

For those who tend a garden or have access to a great farmers market, this salad is for you. It's a celebration of fresh ingredients, not overly manipulated, just dressed up and served. My preference for sweet onions is the Texas 1015, which has been named the official state onion of Texas. It's available from March through September and has a mild nature and sweetness that's perfect for this type of raw preparation.

Chipotle Mashed Potatoes

5 pounds russet potatoes,
    roughly cut

1 stick unsalted butter

$^1/_4$ cup sour cream

1 cup heavy cream

2 ounces ($^1/_2$ can) chipotle
    peppers in adobo sauce

3 $^1/_2$ teaspoons kosher salt

$^1/_2$ teaspoon freshly ground
    black pepper

Rinse the potatoes well (I leave on the skins), then place in a large pot and fill with cold water. Bring to a boil and cook until the potatoes are soft; the time will depend on how small you cut the potatoes but can be anywhere from 10 to 45 minutes. Once cooked, drain the water out and return potatoes to the warm pot.

In a separate pot, bring the butter, sour cream, heavy cream, chipotles, salt, and pepper to a simmer, then puree with a stick blender. Add the pureed mixture to the hot potatoes and mash quickly with a stick masher. Stir once to combine, but do not overmix or the potatoes will become gluey.

Serves 8–10

Be careful when handling chipotles, since they have quite a little kick to them. The smoky flavor and spicy notes that they add to these potatoes make this dish a big hit with most guests, but keep an eye on the heat level if you are serving kids. The real trick to great mashed potatoes is to pour the flavor agents over the hot potatoes right after they have cooked and mash them into the mix.

Braised Southern Greens

4 strips bacon

4 cloves garlic, minced

$1/2$ small onion, diced

2 pounds greens (turnip,
  mustard, chard, collard,
  and beet all work well)

$1^1/2$ teaspoons kosher salt

$1/2$ teaspoon freshly ground
  black pepper

$1/3$ cup dry white wine

$1/4$ cup cider vinegar

Dice the bacon and heat in a soup pot until most of the fat has been rendered. Add the garlic and onion and cook until the onion has softened. Clean the greens well in cold water, and remove any heavy stems. Add the greens to the pot along with the salt and pepper, then pour in the white wine. Cover with a lid and cook on low heat for 15–20 minutes. Remove the lid and pour in the vinegar just prior to serving.

Serves 6–8

The unique aroma of braising greens fills many southern kitchens today, as well as the childhood memories of many Texans. There are so many different types of greens to choose from that I usually combine three or four different varieties for complexity and balance. Be sure to wash all greens thoroughly and plunge them deep into cold water to remove any sandy particles. The tough stems of most greens, though flavorful, are a bit too fibrous and stringy to enjoy in this dish, so I usually discard them. I like to serve greens along with a bottle of pepper vinegar or hot sauce for an extra little kick.

Bacon-Laced Black Beans

1 pound black turtle beans,
    rinsed under cold water

1 large yellow onion,
    diced and divided

4 strips bacon, diced

3 cloves garlic, minced

1 1/2 teaspoons salt

1/2 teaspoon freshly ground
    black pepper

Place the beans and half of the chopped onion in a saucepot with just enough cold water to cover. Soak in the fridge overnight, then simmer for approximately 1 hour (do not drain), just until the beans become soft. Strain the liquid into a separate bowl and keep it for later.

In a separate pot, render the bacon, then add the remaining onion and the garlic. Sauté until the onion has softened; then pour the beans and 1 cup of their cooking liquid into the pot. Puree the mix with a stick blender until smooth.

Serves 8–10

When cooking with black beans, it's extremely important to pick through the beans ahead of time to remove any debris or small stones. Black beans are notorious for harboring little extras like this. I like to garnish these beans with either additional bacon bits or yellow Pico de Gallo (see page 20; substitute yellow tomatoes). The cool, spicy, crisp pico is a perfect contrast to the rich, earthy, smooth bean puree.

Roasted Fall Root Vegetables

4 pounds assorted root vegetables
(purple potatoes, sweet
potatoes, rutabagas, turnips,
pearl onions, parsnips)

1 1/2 teaspoons kosher salt

1/2 teaspoon freshly ground
black pepper

2 tablespoons olive oil

1 tablespoon chopped fresh thyme

2 sprigs fresh rosemary, leaves
removed and stems discarded

Peel the vegetables and cut into rough pieces, all close to the same size so they will cook at about the same rate. Place them all in a mixing bowl and season with salt and pepper. Add oil and herbs and toss to coat well.

Preheat oven to 500 degrees. Spread out vegetables on a baking sheet. Cook for 15 minutes in the oven, stirring every 5 minutes. Vegetables should be well browned and cooked through.

Serves 8–10

Once fall arrives and the root veggies dominate the local growing scene, I love to mix and match different flavors for roasted dishes like this. This kind of mix fills the entire house with familiar smells of autumn and works well as a side for almost any roasted or grilled meats.

Bacon and Boursin Grits

3 strips thick-cut bacon, diced,
    plus more for garnish

$^1/_2$ cup chopped onion

1 teaspoon butter

$^1/_2$ teaspoon kosher salt

1 cup heavy cream

1 cup chicken stock

$^1/_2$ cup white corn grits

1 package Boursin cheese with
    Garlic and Fine Herbs

$^1/_2$ teaspoon chopped fresh thyme

$^1/_2$ teaspoon chopped fresh
    flat-leaf parsley

$^1/_2$ teaspoon chopped fresh oregano

Pinch freshly ground black pepper

In a medium saucepot, render the bacon until just beginning to crisp, then add the onion, butter, and salt. Cook just until the onion becomes soft. Pour in the cream and stock. Bring to a simmer, then whisk in the grits and simmer on low for 20 minutes (5 minutes if using instant grits). Once the grits have cooked and absorbed most of the liquid, fold in the cheese and all remaining ingredients.

Serves 4–6

 I use stone ground grits from the Homestead Gristmill for all of my grits recipes because they just plain taste better than the instant stuff. They have a larger cut and take about 20 minutes to cook, but the end product is fantastic. Instant grits will work and they won't taste bad, but going the extra mile for artisan stone-ground is well worth the effort. I also like to garnish the top of this dish with a few extra crumbled bacon bits.

Blue Corn and Blue Cheese Grits

1 cup chopped onion

3 cloves garlic, minced

1 tablespoon butter

1 cup chicken stock

$1/2$ teaspoon kosher salt

1 cup heavy cream

$1/2$ cup blue corn grits

2 ounces Brazos Valley blue
cheese, cut into rough pieces,
plus more for garnish

2 heaping tablespoons soft
Gorgonzola cheese

2 tablespoons grated
Parmesan cheese

In a saucepan, sweat the onion and garlic in butter until the onion softens. Add the chicken stock, salt, and cream and bring to a simmer. Whisk in the grits and simmer on low for 18–20 minutes, until the grits have cooked and absorbed most of the liquid. Add in all of the cheeses and stir while melting. Serve hot with a small crumble of blue cheese on top.

Serves 4–6.

I like to use two different types of blue cheese in this recipe just for a little balance. The Brazos Valley cheese is very intensely flavored and sharp and is my predominant flavor, while the Gorgonzola is creamier and milder. The rich, rustic nature of these grits makes a perfect complement to beef and game and really pairs well with full-bodied Cabernet.

Southwestern Skillet Potatoes

5 pounds potatoes, peeled,
    diced large

Oil for deep-frying

3 tablespoons vegetable oil

6 tablespoons butter

1 large onion, diced

6 cloves garlic, minced

2 poblano peppers, stems and
    seeds removed, diced

1/2 pound tasso ham, diced small

1 cup heavy cream

1 tablespoon kosher salt

4–5 dashes hot sauce (I prefer
    Crystal Hot Sauce for this one)

This is a large recipe and will need to be done in batches unless you have a very large skillet. Begin by frying the cubed potatoes in a deep fryer at 350 degrees until golden brown on all sides. Drain on paper towels and keep warm until ready for the next step. A bread warming drawer works well for this, or a 200-degree oven. In a hot skillet, add a touch of vegetable oil and butter and sauté the onion, garlic, peppers, and ham until the onion becomes very soft and lightly browned. Add the potatoes and pour in the heavy cream. Reduce on high heat until the cream thickens. Season, stir, and serve immediately.

Serves 12

 Meat and potatoes are staples of Texas cooking, but that doesn't mean either one has to be boring. These are some of the most intensely flavored potatoes that I know how to fix, and they always end up being big crowd pleasers. It takes a little work, but these skillet potatoes are well worth the extra effort.

Sweet and Spicy Pecans

1 pound Texas pecan halves

1 cup powdered sugar

1 tablespoon plus 1 1/2 teaspoons
Texas Red Dirt Rub Creole Blend

1 tablespoon plus 1 1/2 teaspoons
chipotle chili powder

1/2 teaspoon cayenne pepper

1 tablespoon Texas honey

Boil pecans for 8 minutes in enough water to cover, then strain. In a mixing bowl, combine the pecans with the rest of the ingredients and toss well to coat. Cover bowl with plastic wrap and let sit for 8 minutes.

Toss to coat one last time, then drop the pecans into a deep fryer set to 300 degrees. Fry until all bubbling subsides, roughly 2 minutes. Remove from the fryer and drain on paper towels briefly, then scatter on a cookie sheet lined with wax paper to dry. Let cool completely, then store in a sealed container.

Makes 4 cups

 These pecans are quite addicting, so be warned! They need to dry on wax paper to avoid sticking to each other. Be sure they are well scattered or they will clump together and stick like glue. Once they have cooled completely, they will get somewhat of a candy shell on the outside and won't stick. They can be kept for quite some time in a sealed container.

Sweet Heat Pumpkin Seeds

4 ounces pepitas (seeds from
   a sugar pumpkin)

$1/4$ cup powdered sugar

2 teaspoons Red Dirt Rub
   Creole Blend

2 teaspoons chipotle chili powder

Boil the seeds for 8 minutes, then strain and place in a mixing bowl. Add all other ingredients and toss to coat well. Cover the bowl and let the seeds sit for 8–10 minutes while the seasonings soak in. Drop the seeds into a fryer set to 300 degrees for $3^{1}/_{2}$ minutes. Scatter on wax paper and let dry. They must be well scattered while drying or the seeds will stick together. Once dry (about 10 minutes) they are ready and can be stored in a sealed container for several days.

Makes 1 cup

 Pumpkin seeds make a good snack on their own, but when given a sweet heat like this, they come alive with great flavor. Be sure that you buy pepitas, or sugar pumpkin seeds, for this recipe. This will not work with seeds scraped from a jack-o-lantern pumpkin.

Somethin' Sweet

It's hard to imagine a great meal that doesn't have at least a little sweet something or other at the end to punctuate it.

Everyone looks forward to dessert a little bit, whether they admit to it or not. Kids always look for desserts first, which makes them easy to bribe. I can still recall the desperate look on my niece Elizabeth's face, both hands propping up her chin while she stared point blank at the huge cake on my wedding day. After painful hours of waiting through our reception, she finally tugged at my tuxedo jacket and summoned the courage to ask, "Uncle Jon, when are you gonna cut that cake so we can eat some?" There's just something about sweets that attracts the human soul.

There is one recipe that I cannot share entirely, even though I've always had a "no secrets" policy in my kitchen. It's my grandmother's recipe for Chocolate Espresso Cake. I'm sorry that I cannot publish exactly how she makes it, but you can find my adapted version on page 219. Other than that, I give away fully and freely all recipes that I've ever come up with. These are some of my favorite desserts that I like to serve to my favorite Texans.

Lemon Pound Cake with Booze-Infused Berries

1 cup butter, softened

3 cups sugar

5 eggs

1/4 cup vegetable oil

1 cup milk

Juice of 2 lemons

1 teaspoon lemon extract

3 cups flour

Using a stand mixer, cream the butter and sugar together for 2 full minutes. While the mixer is running, add the eggs one at a time and fully incorporate each. Combine the wet ingredients in a separate bowl and whisk. Alternately add flour and wet ingredients (ending with flour) to the mixer while it is running on low-medium, until all ingredients are incorporated. Pour into a greased and floured Bundt pan and bake at 300 degrees for 1 hour, or until a skewer inserted into the middle of the cake comes out clean. Let cool for 15 minutes, then remove from the pan. Top with warm Booze-Infused Berries and serve.

Serves 8–10

BOOZE-INFUSED BERRIES

1 teaspoon water

1/4 cup sugar

1/2 cup blueberries

1/2 cup blackberries

1/2 cup raspberries

2 tablespoons dark rum

2 tablespoons Grand Marnier

Place the sugar and water in a clean pan and heat until the sugar begins to melt and just starts turning light brown. Add the berries and the alcohol. Be careful when adding alcohol, as it may flame up. Never add alcohol directly from a bottle to a hot pan, always pour into a cup or glass first, then into the pan. Stir lightly until the berries have just begun to break apart and form a dark syrup. Pour the mixture over the cake, or spoon a little over each slice when plated.

Makes 1 1/2 cups

This cake is one of my all-time favorite desserts. The texture is dense; yet the cake remains moist and tender. The berry mixture soaks in perfectly, for a sinfully rich and decadent experience. Any leftover cake makes a delicious breakfast slice to help jump-start a long day.

Margarita Key Lime Pie

GRAHAM CRACKER CRUST

1 package (9 crackers total)
    graham crackers
3 tablespoons melted butter

KEY LIME FILLING

4 egg yolks
1/4 cup plus 2 tablespoons freshly
    squeezed key lime juice
1 (14-ounce) can sweetened
    condensed milk

TOPPING

Zest of 1 orange
Zest of 1 lime
2 tablespoons kosher salt
1 tablespoon plus 1 1/2
    teaspoons sugar

For the graham cracker crust, crush the crackers into crumbs, mix well with melted butter and spread across the bottom and up the sides of a pie tin. A food processor is generally the best tool for crushing and mixing the crackers.

For the key lime filling, preheat oven to 350 degrees. Mix all ingredients together with a whisk until very well blended. Pour into the crust and bake for 15 minutes, until slightly firm.

For the topping, Place the orange and lime zest on a paper towel and press to release most of the liquid. Place the zest, sugar, and salt in a food processor and pulse a few times until well mixed. Sprinkle over the finished pie to create that unmistakable margarita flavor.

Serves 6–8

 The key to great key lime pie is using freshly squeezed key lime juice. Key limes are smaller than standard limes (about the size of golf balls), and they usually contain plenty of seeds, so juicing them can be quite a chore but well worth it! The juice has a different acidity and flavor that cannot be obtained from any other type of lime or frozen product. A great key lime pie is simple and celebrates the unique flavor of this fruit. I like to add the sweet and salty zest topping to re-create the flavors of a perfect margarita.

Sweet Pecan Biscuits with Cactus Jelly

3 cups flour
$^1/_2$ cup sugar
2 tablespoons baking powder
Pinch of salt
$^1/_2$ pound butter, cut into cubes,
 plus more for serving
1 $^1/_4$ cups buttermilk
$^1/_2$ cup chopped pecans
Cactus Jelly, purchased

Combine all of the dry ingredients and mix well. Cut the butter into the flour mixture by hand or with a dough cutter. Mix until the flour takes on a "wet sand" texture. Add the buttermilk and pecans and mix just until the dough comes together, but no further. Roll out the dough 2 inches thick on a floured surface. Cut the biscuits into circles and bake on a greased sheet in a preheated 350-degree oven for 10–12 minutes, until golden brown on top. Serve with soft butter and cactus jelly.

Makes 12–14 biscuits

The jelly for these biscuits is made from the fruit of prickly pear cactus. When the fruit is ripe, the flavor is exceptionally sweet and the color tends to be an electric hot pink. The tangy sweet jelly is available from many producers in Texas and across the Southwest and makes a perfect accompaniment to sweet biscuits for breakfast.

Blueberries Flambé

½ cup sugar

2 cups fresh blueberries

Juice and zest of 1 lemon

¼ cup dark rum

2 tablespoons Barcardi 151 rum

2 tablespoons Grand Marnier

1 recipe Sweet Pecan Biscuits
(see page 202)

1 pint Blue Bell vanilla ice cream

Add the sugar to a preheated sauté pan. Once the sugar melts, watch closely. As soon as it begins to turn light brown, add the blueberries. Stir with a heat-resistant utensil until the blueberries begin to burst and a dark purple syrup begins to form. Add the zest and juice, then all of the alcohols. Do not pour the alcohols directly from their bottles, but rather pour first into a glass, then into the pan. Flame the pan and swirl it until the flame dies out. Cut the sweet biscuits in half and place the halves in individual bowls; top each with a scoop of ice cream. Spoon a mixture of the berries and syrup over and serve.

Serves 6–8

 Nothing finishes a great dinner party and impresses guests quite like an open-flame, tableside dessert. Blueberries are extremely plentiful in Texas and make the most beautiful dark purple syrup that works perfectly when soaked into a sweet biscuit. Be sure to practice your flambé technique at least once before attempting it in front of people; once you have some confidence, this dish is a guaranteed winner.

Berry Bread Pudding with Bourbon Sauce

4 cups dry bread, cut into large cubes
　　(white French bread works well)
$1/2$ cup chopped pecans
$1/4$ cup raisins
$1/2$ cup dried cherries
$1/4$ cup dried blueberries
5 large eggs
$2 1/4$ cups half-and-half
$1/2$ cup sugar
1 teaspoon ground cinnamon
1 teaspoon vanilla extract

Butter a square nonstick baking dish and add in the cubes of bread. Sprinkle in the nuts and the fruits. In a large mixing bowl, whisk together all remaining ingredients and then pour over the bread and fruits. Allow the mixture to soak in the refrigerator for at least 30 minutes before baking.

Preheat oven to 375 degrees. Bake pudding in a water bath (optional) for 45–55 minutes. Check for doneness by jiggling to see if the center is cooked. When the center is cooked all the way through, remove from oven, scoop into bowls for serving, and top with warm Bourbon Sauce.

Serves 4–6

BOURBON SAUCE

4 tablespoons ($1/2$ stick) butter
$1/2$ cup sugar
$1/4$ cup heavy cream
$1/3$ cup bourbon
Pinch of salt

Bring all ingredients to a light simmer, stir until the sugar is melted, and serve.

Makes 1 pint

Bread pudding is a great dessert to make for a large crowd since it takes a while to bake but can be served very quickly once done. It's incredibly rich and decadent, perfect for those special occasions when it's time to pull out the stops and have a great time. Though it works very well with just a heavy dose of the Bourbon Sauce, I sometimes add a scoop of rich vanilla ice cream as well.

Cream-Filled Sopaipillas with White Chocolate Sauce

2 cups flour
1 teaspoon baking powder
$1/2$ teaspoon iodized salt
2 tablespoons vegetable shortening
$3/4$ cup warm water (90–100 degrees)
Oil for deep-frying

CINNAMON SUGAR

$1/3$ cup sugar
1 teaspoon cinnamon

CREAM FILLING

1 cup milk
$1 1/2$ cups heavy cream
$1/2$ teaspoon cinnamon
5 large egg yolks
$1/2$ cup sugar
1 tablespoon cornstarch
2 tablespoons butter
1 teaspoon vanilla extract
$1/4$ cup white chocolate morsels

WHITE CHOCOLATE SAUCE

$3/4$ cup white chocolate morsels
$1/2$ cup plus 1 tablespoon heavy cream
3 tablespoons dark rum

Place the first three dry ingredients in an electric stand mixer with the paddle attachment in place. Drop in soft cubes of the shortening and turn on low. Mix until the ingredients are well blended, then slowly drizzle in the warm water on medium speed until the dough forms a ball. Turn out onto a board and knead lightly by hand, then let the dough rest for 20–25 minutes. Roll out to $1/8$ inch thick, then cut into squares, triangles, circles, or stars. Deep-fry in 375-degree vegetable oil for approximately 3–4 minutes, turning once. Drain on paper towels and coat with cinnamon sugar, then puncture lightly with the tip of a knife and fill with cream filling using a pastry bag and star tip.

Makes 10–12 small or 4–6 large sopaipillas

For the cream filling: Combine all ingredients in a small saucepot and bring to a gentle boil while whisking. Once the mixture boils, reduce to low and simmer for 1 full minute, then cool. Transfer to a bowl and cover with plastic wrap placed directly on the surface to avoid a skin forming. Place the mixture into a pastry bag with a metal tip and pipe it into the sopaipillas as a creamy filling.

Makes $2 1/2$ cups

For the sauce: Combine all ingredients in a sauté pan and warm gently, stirring, until the chocolate is melted. Pour over the sopaipillas as a glaze.

Makes $1 1/4$ cups

The sopaipilla is every kid's favorite part about eating out in Mexican restaurants. This deep-fried bread arrives at the table hot and steaming, with plenty of honey to drizzle over the top. I tend to go overboard with sopaipillas, stuffing them with cream filling and making a white chocolate glaze, rather than the traditional pure honey, but I have yet to hear one complaint on these babies.

Funnel Cakes

2 cups flour

1 teaspoon baking powder

1 teaspoon salt

1 tablespoon sugar

1 1/2 cups whole milk

2 eggs

1/2 teaspoon vanilla

6 tablespoons melted butter

Oil for deep-frying

1/2 cup powdered sugar mixed
   with 1/2 teaspoon cinnamon

Sift flour, baking powder and salt into a mixing bowl. Add sugar and stir to blend. In a stand mixer using the whip attachment, blend the milk, eggs, and vanilla. Add the dry ingredients and mix until the batter is light and fluffy. Drizzle in the melted butter last, and mix until completely incorporated.

Heat oil to 350 degrees in a deep fryer or other heavy-bottomed pan.

Pour about 1/4 to 1/3 cup batter, more or less, into a funnel while holding a finger over the bottom to keep it from leaking out. This can also be done using a pastry bag or a ziplock bag with one corner cut out. Pour or squirt the batter quickly into the oil, forming a crisscross pattern. Fry for approximately 1 minute per side, or until golden brown, then drain on paper towels and top with powdered cinnamon sugar.

Makes approximately 8 cakes

The funnel cake is a Texas tradition usually associated with big special events like the state fair, the rodeo, or a trip to Six Flags. I have no idea how it started or who made it first, but fried sweet dough dusted with liberal amounts of powdered cinnamon sugar is a sinful pleasure, to be sure. This is the perfect recipe for turning any ordinary parent into an immortal hero at kids' parties. Funnel cakes are indulgent to say the least, but worthy of the trouble down to each finger-licking bite.

Dessert Tostadas

6 (6- or 8-inch) flour tortillas
Oil for deep-frying
1 teaspoon ground cinnamon
$^{1}/_{3}$ cup sugar
Chocolate Ganache
$^{1}/_{4}$ cup white chocolate shavings
$^{1}/_{4}$ cup chopped pecans
Seeds of 1 pomegranate

Heat oil to 350 degrees in a deep fryer or other heavy-bottomed pan. Fry tortillas one at a time, turning once, until they crisp and become golden on both sides. Remove and drain on paper towels. Coat on both sides with a mixture of the cinnamon and sugar as soon as they come out of the oil. Spread a generous amount of Chocolate Ganache on each one, then top with a sprinkling of white chocolate shavings, chopped pecans, and pomegranate seeds.

Serves 6

CHOCOLATE GANACHE

1 cup heavy cream
12 ounces semisweet chocolate morsels
$^{1}/_{2}$ teaspoon ancho chili powder
2 tablespoons bourbon

Heat all ingredients together gently in a saucepan until the chocolate is fully melted. Cool to room temperature, then spread over the tostada crisps.

Makes 2$^{1}/_{2}$ cups

These non-traditional tostadas are a fun and creative dessert sure to be enjoyed by kids and adults alike. I sometimes. cut smaller circles out of the tortillas and serve these little flavor-packed crisps more like the size of little nachos, but bigger sizes work just as well. Don't be afraid of the chili powder in the chocolate: it's earthy, robust, and complex without adding enough heat to deter any kids from enjoying it.

It can be fun to set up a little build-your-own tostado station for parties and let guests pile their tostadas high with any number of different toppings, such as chopped nuts, sprinkles, fruits, or small candies.

Mexican Wedding Cookies

$^1/_2$ cup chopped almonds

8 ounces butter

$^1/_2$ cup sugar

2 teaspoons pure vanilla extract

1 teaspoon bourbon

1 teaspoon dark rum

2 cups flour

$^1/_2$ cup chopped pecans

1 cup powdered sugar

Preheat oven to 350 degrees and toast the almonds on a baking sheet for a few minutes, just until they begin to get light brown; then remove and let cool.

In a stand mixer, cream the butter and sugar until smooth and creamy. Add the liquids and mix thoroughly. Add the flour and nuts and mix until well combined. Scrape the dough from the bowl and place on a floured board. Roll the cookies in approximately 1-inch balls using floured hands; place on a baking sheet sprayed lightly with nonstick spray, or lined with parchment paper.

Turn the oven down to 325 degrees and bake the cookies for 15–20 minutes, or until light golden brown. Transfer to a rack and let cool for 30 minutes. Place the powdered sugar in a mixing bowl, drop in a few cookies at a time, and shake the bowl gently to coat the cookies in the powdered sugar.

Makes 24 (1-ounce) cookies

These little treats are crispy and sweet, even if just a little messy on the fingers. Different recipes may call for the addition of different nuts or even some chopped dried fruit, and the shapes can vary from mini torpedoes to crescent moons. I prefer just the simple nuts and round cookies, stacked high on a nice platter with a little extra powdered sugar sprinkled on for garnish.

Pumpkin Cheesecake with Bourbon Whipped Cream

GRAHAM CRACKER CRUST

1 package (9 crackers total)
   graham crackers

3 tablespoons melted butter

CHEESECAKE

5 eggs

1 (15-ounce) can pumpkin puree

2 teaspoons cinnamon

1/2 teaspoon nutmeg

1 teaspoon allspice

1 teaspoon ginger

3 pounds cream cheese,
   room temperature

1 1/2 cups sugar

2 tablespoons brown sugar

1/2 teaspoon vanilla extract

BOURBON WHIPPED CREAM

2 teaspoons powdered sugar

1/2 teaspoon brown sugar

1/2 teaspoon ground cinnamon

3 tablespoons bourbon

2 cups heavy cream

For the crust: In a food processor, crush the crackers into crumbs and mix well with melted butter. Spread the crumbs evenly across the bottom of a springform pan but not up the sides at all.

For the cheesecake: In a stand mixer, combine all ingredients and whip together until uniform and smooth. Begin by mixing slowly, then gradually increase the speed until the mixture is free of all lumps.

Pour the batter over the crumbs. Bake in a preheated 325-degree oven in a water bath (optional) for approximately 45 minutes, or until the cake is set. To check for doneness, lightly jiggle the cake; if the middle jiggles, the cake is not done; check again in 5–10 minutes. Once the cake is done, remove and let cool. Separate the cake from the pan by running a paring knife around the inside edges of the springform, then release the pan and remove the cake. Cut into slices with a warm knife and top with bourbon-spiked whipped cream.

Serves 14–16

For the whipped cream: Begin by placing the mixing bowl of an electric mixer in the freezer for 10 minutes. Cream whips better when cold. Dissolve the sugars and cinnamon in the bourbon. Pour the cream into the cold bowl. Begin whipping on medium speed, then increase the speed gradually until the cream begins to thicken. Pour in the bourbon and sugar mixture and continue whipping until the cream reaches a stiff peak stage.

Makes 3 cups

This dessert is the number-one fan favorite of my family every Thanksgiving. The pumpkin adds a certain creamy nature to an already rich cheesecake that's simply over-the-top indulgent when topped with spiked whipped cream. Most of the kids even get to enjoy a little Bourbon Whipped Cream, which usually ensures a better afternoon nap than normal.

Be careful when buying pumpkin puree in the can, as many come with an abundance of spice and sugar already mixed in. A little experimenting with different brands may serve well in the final product.

GiGi's Amaretto Chocolate Cake

12 ounces semisweet chocolate morsels
1 1/2 cups sugar
3 sticks (12 ounces) butter
1/2 cup Amaretto liqueur
1/4 cup liquid coffee, French Roast
6 eggs

Melt the chocolate, sugar and butter together gently over a double boiler (a mixing bowl over simmering water). Add the liquids and mix together well. Using an electric mixer, beat the mixture for 2 minutes, then add the eggs one at a time and beat until all are fully incorporated. Pour the batter into a heavily greased springform pan and bake in a 350-degree preheated oven for 40 minutes. When done, let cool completely in the refrigerator before removing from the pan. The center of the cake should sink slightly. Fill the center with Amaretto-Spiked Whipped Cream and cut.

AMARETTO-SPIKED WHIPPED CREAM
1 cup heavy whipping cream
1 1/2 tablespoons Amaretto liqueur
2 tablespoons powdered sugar

Combine all ingredients in a mixing bowl and refrigerate for 1 hour. Whip until the cream forms stiff peaks.

Serves 6–8

My grandmother, age 96, gave me an index card with a handwritten recipe for Chocolate Espresso Cake that is out of this world, but I had to promise to give her credit whenever I make it and not publish the complete contents. Gigi, this is your credit, and I've changed the recipe slightly and added a topping of Amaretto-Spiked Whipped Cream as a garnish. Gigi told me that the recipe was not actually hers originally, that she got it from one of her dear friends, Anne. I later found out that Anne was Anne Lindbergh, wife of Charles Lindbergh, an old pilot buddy of my grandfather's. I love the story almost as much as the cake itself. This cake comes out with a lightly crispy crust on top and a gooey chocolate center that's somewhat messy but packed with rich flavor. Be sure to let the cake chill in the fridge for quite a while before trying to remove it from the pan. It's even a good idea to make this cake the night before and remove it the next day.

Index

⭐ Metric Conversion Chart ⭐

Volume Measurements		Weight Measurements		Temperature Conversion	
U.S.	METRIC	U.S.	METRIC	FAHRENHEIT	CELSIUS
1 teaspoon	5 ml	1/2 ounce	15 g	250	120
1 tablespoon	15 ml	1 ounce	30 g	300	150
1/4 cup	60 ml	3 ounces	90 g	325	160
1/3 cup	75 ml	4 ounces	115 g	350	180
1/2 cup	125 ml	8 ounces	225 g	375	190
2/3 cup	150 ml	12 ounces	350 g	400	200
3/4 cup	175 ml	1 pound	450 g	425	220
1 cup	250 ml	2 1/4 pounds	1 kg	450	230